THE WAY OF THE RIGHTEOUS
IN THE MUCK OF LIFE

THE WAY OF THE RIGHTEOUS
IN THE MUCK OF LIFE

Psalms 1–12

Dale Ralph Davis

CHRISTIAN
FOCUS

Copyright © Dale Ralph Davis

ISBN 978-1-84550-581-3

10 9 8 7 6 5 4 3 2 1

First Published in 2010,
Reprinted in 2011 (twice)
by
Christian Focus Publications Ltd.,
Geanies House, Fearn, Ross-shire,
IV20 1TW, Scotland, Great Britain
www.christianfocus.com

Cover design by
Daniel Van Straaten

Printed by Bell & Bain, Glasgow

Contents

To Frances Adams,

family,

friend,

follower of Jesus

Preface

My father once remarked that when the Lord's people come to the Lord's house they often come dragging heavy burdens; hence, he said, he usually tried to include something in his preaching that might prove heartening to them. 'Comfort, comfort my people, says your God' (Isa. 40:1). And often the Lord's people have found the balm of Gilead flowing from the Psalms. Hence one of the reasons for these expositions—a few of the saints might be fortified.

But why deal with only the first twelve psalms? Because there are one hundred and fifty of them! When preaching from larger biblical books I will often treat only a chunk of the whole book at a time, leave the book for a while, then come back to it later and tackle another segment. I wanted to give our people a taste of the psalms, and so I thought a 'Psalm Sampler' focusing on Psalms 1–12 would fill the bill. What follows are those expositions, which were almost entirely Sunday evening sermons preached to the congregation of Woodland Presbyterian Church. I have not tried to hide the sermonic form, and I have not 'messed with' formal footnoting. The translations provided are my own. I am aware of some repetition which occurs, which, I think, is because sometimes the psalmist 'harps' on the same point.

Two matters call for attention. One is the use of 'Yahweh.' Whenever most of our English translations read 'the LORD' (with 'Lord' in small caps), they indicate that they are translating the covenant name of God, the consonants of which are YHWH, with 'Yahweh' being about the closest we'll probably get with pronunciation. That name was 'explained' in Exodus 3:14-15 as shorthand for the strange 'I am who I am,' or better, 'I will be what I will be.' One must simply remember that in Exodus 3:12 Yahweh had specified what kind of 'being' he is talking about—'But I will be *with you*' (my emphasis). So Exodus 3:14 means 'I will be present is what I will be.' In light of verse 12, God does not here stress his being or existence so much as his presence. And 'Yahweh' captures and summarizes that thought—he is the God who will be present to be all that his people need him to be. 'Yahweh' means the God who is present to help. I don't expect to replace 'the LORD' in popular Christian usage. But 'Yahweh' is a personal name, while 'the LORD' is a title. 'Wife' is my spouse's 'title,' and I suppose I could call her that, but I much prefer 'Barbara,' which is her name. By the same token some of us prefer 'Yahweh'—there's a devotional warmth in a personal name that a title can't convey.

The second matter involves a criticism some will have of these expositions. I do not take a 'Christological' approach and explain these psalms as speaking of Jesus (unless they do, e.g., Pss. 2 and 8). Why is this? Because I do not think Jesus wants me to do so. Some insist that Jesus insists in Luke 24 (vv. 25-7, 44-7) that every Old Testament passage speaks of him in some way. That, I am convinced, over-reads (and misreads) the passage. Jesus explained to the disciples 'in all the scriptures' the things concerning himself (v. 27), and he referred to all things written about him 'in the law of Moses and the prophets and the psalms' (v. 44). Note the 'in.' Jesus did not say every Old Testament passage spoke of him; he rather took the apostles through the plethora of passages in all parts of the Old Testament that did speak of him or point to him in some way. (For a fuller discussion, see my *The Word Became Fresh* [Christian Focus, 2006], 134–8).

PSALM 1

1 How blessed the man who
    does not walk in the counsel of the wicked
    and does not stand in the way of sinners
    and does not sit in the seat of scoffers;
2 but his delight is in Yahweh's torah,
  and in his torah he meditates day and night;

3 and he shall be like a tree,
    planted by streams of water,
    that yields its fruit in its time,
    and its leaves never wither;
    and everything that he does prospers.
4 The wicked are not like that!
  But like chaff that wind drives away.

5 Therefore the wicked will not stand in the judgment,
  nor will sinners stand in the congregation of the righteous;
6 for Yahweh knows the way of the righteous,
  but the way of the wicked will perish.

First Things

I was looking over the sports page of the newspaper. It was fall and American college football was in full swing. Certain soon-to-be-played games were listed with several sports writers' predictions of the winners. I was living in the deep south (where I still live) and the first game listed was the Alabama/Ole Miss game (the latter is the popular way of saying 'The University of Mississippi'). There was another game between Penn State and Ohio State, but it appeared far down the list. Now why was that? Penn State and Ohio State were two big football programs, two 'national'-level teams. Why so far down the list? Because this was the deep south and to those living there Alabama and Ole Miss was the big game that week, and, to be brutally truthful, unless someone was a northern 'transplant' who was fixated on one's old team, no one in the south really cared a lick if Penn State and Ohio State even played. The first listing was first because that was the most important one.

It might be a bit like that with the Psalms. Why is Psalm 1 Psalm 1? Why is it placed here? In the church today we need such help with praise—so why isn't Psalm 150 Psalm 1? And how we need to learn worship—so why isn't Psalm 100 (or 95) Psalm 1? What could be more winsome than plastering the mercy of God across the front page of the Psalter—so why isn't Psalm 103 at the first? Maybe we need to show how attuned the psalms are to human need and troubles—so why isn't Psalm 73 Psalm 1? Or with the break-down in family life maybe Psalm 128 should be here? Or, perhaps first off we need a grand view of the majesty and wonder of God, and we think Psalm 139 should be Psalm 1.

So why is Psalm 1 Psalm 1? Because it packs a matter of such supreme importance. Here two ways, two humanities, two destinies are clearly spelled out. Jesus summed up the concern of Psalm 1 in Matthew 7:13-14 (ESV):

> Enter by the narrow gate. For the gate is wide and the way is easy that leads to destruction, and those who enter by it are many. For the gate is narrow and the way is hard that leads to life, and those who find it are few.

Psalm 1 depicts this in terse, stark black and white, as if announcing, 'Let the clarity begin!' The psalm is saying to you: *Nothing is so crucial as your belonging to the congregation of the righteous.*

The psalm contrasts the righteous and the wicked. We will not ignore the contrast but will develop the teaching from the angle of the righteous or believing person.

The direction of the believer's life

Notice first what the psalm highlights about the direction of the believer's life (vv. 1-2). Here the psalm shows where the righteous man gets his signals for living—what drives him and moves him and leads him along.

And, as if he has no concern whatever for decent marketing, the psalmist begins with the *negative* (v. 1). The righteous man is described by what he shuns. The happy man (or, the man enjoying God's blessing) is the separated man, a man who is not in neutral but who has a bias against evil in all its forms. The three clauses are meant to say that the righteous man rejects the totality of evil. However, *a la* Derek Kidner, we can categorize these matters a bit. The 'counsel' of the wicked has to do with a way of thinking, with forming plans, with a mind-set and outlook. The 'way' of sinners suggests their behavior, their actions and practices. The 'seat' of the scoffers implies a kind of belonging, where one settles most comfortably perhaps with the scathing unbelief that wants no truck with godliness and faithfulness. If we look at these clauses as what is congenial to the wicked man, then we see the cues he follows (counsel), the direction he takes (way), and the company he enjoys (seat, etc.).

So...how happy the man who does not.... He is counter-cultural. He is, in a word, different. He is not just a nice, easy-going, tolerant chap who likes to share a Löwenbräu with you. There's a difference between the righteous man here and what my culture calls a 'good old boy.' He resists the vacuum-cleaner power-moves that evil puts on him. Mardy Grothe tells of a long-lived lady who, when asked what was the best thing about being 104, replied, 'No peer pressure.' But the righteous man in verse 1 is not 104 and he meets plenty of peer pressure. It may cost him. But the righteous man is the one who does not go with the flow.

We must always remember that the lure of the wicked and sinners and scoffers does not usually appear in its grossest form. It may come in rather bump-a-long fashion from teachers or friends or family—or spouses; it simply suggests that if you don't think this way, you will not be thought sharp; if you don't act this way, you will not be 'cool'; if you don't laugh at what we mock, we don't want any part of you. Verse 1 is not merely description but warning, a sort of Old Testament Romans 12:2: 'Don't let the world around you squeeze you into its own mould' (Phillips).

But there is the *positive* side of the believer's direction (v. 2). What leads him to renounce all the 'appeals' of verse 1? To turn and walk away from it all? The pursuit of pleasure! He does it because he cares more for his pleasure than for his pressures! 'But his delight....' Note that last word. You are going to take your signals from somewhere, and he takes his from the torah of Yahweh rather than from the counsel of the wicked.

What is this 'torah'? The word is usually translated 'law,' but that gives too confining a notion of it. Even when we use 'law' of the Pentateuch (first five books of the Old Testament) we know it includes narrative (e.g., Genesis) and exhortation (e.g., Deuteronomy) and not merely legal directives. 'Torah' means teaching, instruction, doctrine. And it can be written down in a 'scripture document' (Josh. 1:8). And here in the first psalm its use may well imply that the 'torah', the teaching of Yahweh, will also include the praises and prayers and cries of the saints put in print here.

Now this torah, this teaching of Yahweh, is his delight. The righteous man's existence is not dullsville; he gets his kicks from pondering Yahweh's will in Yahweh's word. His pleasure is clear not simply in some feeling he has for Yahweh's word but in his *preoccupation* with it: 'and in his torah he meditates day and night.' The verb seems to carry the idea of muttering or murmuring in an undertone. If done with a written document, it reflects a vocal activity rather than a mere silent reading (which we westerners seem to prefer). It would be something like the way my mother-in-law used to read a newspaper article—she would whisper the words as she read them. This 'meditating' might be similar to what I do when I (un-male-like) have to stop and ask directions. A service or petrol station attendant may give me directions, then I repeat them to him/her to confirm that I have them correct, mutter them to myself once or twice as I walk back to our vehicle, and then repeat them to my wife when I get in. One has to work it in, so to speak. That is what one is to do with Yahweh's torah— and one is to do this 'day and night', that is, regularly and consistently.

Sometimes it seems like this torah-meditating is all that keeps Christians afloat. When I was fourteen our family moved—only 55 miles, but it was not only a different location but a different culture. I was not comfortable in my new high school, in fact thought it close to misery incarnate. The Lord seemed to be awakening me to the seriousness of my profession of faith and my new school and surroundings seemed decidedly hostile or indifferent to a young Christian's commitment. As I look back, I'm sure I exaggerated the problem, but in my mind every day was a battle in seeking to live for Christ in an unfriendly world. But every morning before dragging myself to the bus stop I could sink my teeth into torah! How the Psalms spoke to my condition. I could take my red ball point pen and underline such assurances as *This I know, that God is for me* (Ps. 56:9) or *in God I trust without a fear—what can man do to me?* (56:11). Meditation in those psalms seemed to put me in the shadow of Yahweh's wings and settle me on the rock of his faithfulness, and faith's fingernails were able to hang on for another day. To be sure, God's word was sheer necessity, but it was also a delight.

So total immersion in the word of Yahweh forms the basis of the believer's life and is his/her pleasure and preoccupation. The 'counsel of the wicked' or the 'torah of Yahweh'—which drives your life?

The description of the believer's life

Secondly, the psalm provides us with the description of the believer's life (vv. 3–4).

My oldest brother, who is a historian, finished his magnum opus on 'Eastern and Western History, Thought and Culture, 1600–1815' and gave us a copy. He digests and covers and analyzes history, politics, and humanities in a massive 800 pages. My wife's response when I showed it to her was: 'Are there any pictures?' No, it was all print; pictures doubtless cost more shekels! But the psalmist says, 'Here, let me give you a couple of pictures.' Ah, a psalm with pictures!

Before the first picture you must notice one connection. You must see that the picture of the blessed man in verse 3 is directly linked to verses 1–2. Verse 3 begins, 'And he shall be...' The 'and' in Hebrew is usually omitted by English translations, but it is important. The psalm is saying that this picture of the blessed man in verse 3 flows out of and is the result of his living out of the word of God in verses 1-2.

Now the picture: the righteous man is 'like a tree' (3a). The text fleshes out the analogy. The righteous man has stability ('planted'), vitality ('by streams of water'), productivity ('gives its fruit'), durability ('does not wither'), and prosperity ('all that he does prospers'). Some might over-read the last clause and ask, 'You mean there are no reversals, no setbacks?' No, you must realize Psalm 1 is what Alec Motyer would call an Apostles' Creed-approach; it's broad-brush here; we'll get to the nasty side later (e.g., Pss. 3, 73); don't expect a psalmist to ruin a fine, succinct summary by cluttering it with howevers and nevertheless. I think stability-with-vitality captures the essence of this picture.

That, by the way, is an interesting combination. We often set those characteristics against each other. We may know creative people who have hardly a whip-stitch of order, and we assume it goes with the turf. 'Oh, she's artsy—you can't expect her to show up on time.' Or someone else is a neat-freak, and because of that we're sure he would never consider a moment of spontaneous fun—not until he showered, shaved, made his bed, paid his bills, washed his breakfast dishes and put his dirty clothes in the hamper. But you've got stability and vitality combined in this blessed man. The one who says no to the world (v. 1) and yes to Yahweh's word (v. 2) is the one who is both rooted and lively (v. 3); his stability is not monotonous and his vitality is not chaotic.

But we might say that's not the whole picture. 'It's not like that with the wicked' (v. 4) introduces a second, contrasting picture. The wicked are like chaff. Go to the threshing-floor; when the farmer's fork scoops up and throws grain into the air, the wind blows the light chaff away. If the tree represents stability and vitality, chaff depicts rootlessness (v. 4) and ruin (vv. 5–6). Look carefully at the text: note how four clauses explain and amplify the picture of the righteous as a tree (v. 3), but only one line depicts the wicked as chaff. Very abrupt. Well, how much can you really say about chaff anyway?

Occasionally someone has the insight to pronounce a 'chaff' estimate on his life. Marvin Olasky (in *Prodigal Press*) tells of Horace Greeley, the editor of the *New York Tribune* for over 30 years. Greeley, who believed man was naturally good, backed the founding of some forty communes during the 1840s, all of which failed. He advocated various other causes, among them 'free love'; he always seemed to be pressing for something new, as if it might usher in a man-made utopia. He was politically crushed when he ran for President in 1872. After the election, he looked back on his life, viewed it as a waste and a sacrifice to one foolish crusade after another. In a statement not long before his death, he wrote: 'I stand naked before my God, the most utterly, hopelessly wretched and undone of all who ever lived. I have done more harm and wrong than any man who ever saw the light of day. And yet I take God to witness that I have never intended to injure or harm anyone. But this is no excuse.' Perhaps the only thing worse than being chaff is to *know* you have been chaff.

But Psalm 92:12–15 gives a quite different picture of the righteous:

The righteous flourish like the palm tree
   and grow like a cedar in Lebanon.
They are planted in the house of Yahweh;
   they flourish in the courts of our God.
They still bear fruit in old age;
   they are ever full of sap and green,
to declare that Yahweh is upright;
   he is my rock,
   and there is no unrighteousness in him (ESV, alt.).

It's the Psalm 1 reflection—planted and still bearing fruit. I think it's true. I can take you to believers who are in their 70s and 80s who will witness to this, who will tell you straight out that God has never stopped giving them stability and keeping them on their feet—and that he still sustains them with life in Jesus. Like a tree...

The destiny of the believer's life

Finally, the psalm points us ahead to the destiny of the believer's life (vv. 5–6). The 'therefore' introducing these verses shows where it is all heading. When verse 5 refers to 'the judgment' it means what we call the final judgment. That is why Psalm 1 is so serious and solemn. Here is no trifle; here is no piddly little religious game that we're playing. It's as if the psalm asks us what we will do when the end comes (cf. Jer. 5:31).

We have friends who are missionaries in Uganda. In a 2007 newsletter they wrote that there are signs all over

Kampala: 'Are you ready for CHOGM?' 'We are ready for CHOGM!' 'Uganda is ready for CHOGM!' CHOGM stands for Commonwealth Heads of Government Meeting, and from the UK the Queen was to come. All over the city they were repairing roads, clearing ditches, cleaning up litter, planting trees and grass—even washing guard rails! Uganda had to be ready. And that is the urgency verse 5 should stir in us: The judgment! Are you ready for the judgment?

Some are not. Note the way the wicked are depicted. They have *no justification*; they 'will not stand in the judgment' (5a); they have *no communion*; 'nor will sinners stand in the congregation of the righteous' (5b)—they are cut off, outside the community of God's flock; and they have *no hope*; 'but the way of the wicked will perish' (6b).

But who are these 'wicked'? The scope of this psalm seems to take in only Israel. Unlike Psalm 2, it is not looking at the pagans or the nations at large. That does not mean there are no wicked among the nations, but only that the primary concern and 'coverage' of Psalm 1 is centered on Israel. It seems to be talking to and about the covenant people. So when the psalm speaks of the 'wicked' (vv. 1, 4, 5, 6) we more naturally—and rightly—assume they are Israelite wicked. You can be numbered outwardly among the people of God and yet be one of the wicked, one of those who 'will not stand' in the judgment. This is the doctrine our Savior teaches in Matthew 7:21–3. There Jesus speaks of 'that day' when apparent disciples will cite their very dynamic ministries as evidence that they are his. Sadly, Jesus answers that one can be sound (calling Jesus 'Lord'), sincere (note the fervent, 'Lord, Lord'), successful (the power-ministries of v. 22)—and lost.

But what of the righteous in this time of the judgment? The only explanation we have here is in verse 6a: 'Yahweh knows the way of the righteous.' The verbal form is a participle and refers to ongoing action: Yahweh continually knows. This does not mean merely that Yahweh knows the road the righteous take, with every twist and turn—though that is true; but it particularly means that 'God is intimately and personally concerned about every step the righteous man takes' (Henry Snaith). If that is true, then it means that the God who cares about every step he takes will care for him as well when he steps into the judgment, and so he will be preserved at the last and not perish.

Faith Cook has left us a marvelous set of mini 'bios' in her *Lives Turned Upside Down*. She tells of Ruth Clark, born in 1741 into a rather well-to-do family. But her father was a speculator and, by the time Ruth was ten, had lost his fortune—and walked out on his family. Ruth then had to become a domestic servant; in fact, she became a superb domestic servant. When 18 she came to work for the Venns, as in Henry Venn, the well-known 18th century evangelical Anglican preacher. In about another decade—which included the earnest address of Mrs. Venn on her death bed—Ruth was converted and continued to serve the Venn household and her community, showing a faith that was alive with the fruit of the Spirit. She outlived Henry Venn and, when her own health broke, she was welcomed into the home of Venn's eldest daughter in Brighton. When 67, she was crossing a street and was knocked to the ground by a speeding horse and cart. This accident brought on a more serious illness and she was in her last days. One of the Venn daughters was visiting her and asked her if she had any doubts about her hope in Christ. Ruth simply confessed,

'Oh no, none. He that has loved me all my life through will not forsake me now. I have no rapturous feelings, but I have no fears or doubts.' She was simply repeating Psalm 1:6a in other words. *He that has loved me all my life through will not forsake me now.* The God who cares about every step his righteous servant takes will surely care for her when the next step is into the judgment. That is one part of the 'last things' that you must be very clear about.

Solemn matters here. The first word of the psalm is 'blessed,' the last is 'perish.' These are first things. Face them now. Make sure you are among the congregation of the righteous. How do you get in? Come to Jesus, who says: 'I am the door; if anyone enters by me, he will be saved, and will go in and out and find pasture' (John 10:9).

PSALM 2

1 Why do the nations rage?
  And why do the peoples keep plotting hopeless plans?
2 Why do the kings of the earth take their stand
  and why do the rulers conspire together
  —against Yahweh and against his Anointed King?
3 'Let us rip off their fetters
  and let's throw off their cords.'

4 The One who sits in the heavens laughs!
  The Lord mocks at them!
5 Then he speaks to them in his wrath,
  yes, he terrifies them in his hot anger:
6 'But **I** have installed my king on Zion, my holy hill.'

7 Let me tell about the decree;
  Yahweh said to me:
  'You are my son; I have begotten you this very day.

8 Ask me, and I will give nations as your inheritance,
   and the ends of the earth for your possession.
9 You will break them with an iron rod,
   you will smash them to pieces like a clay pot.'

10 And now, you kings! Wise up!
   Accept instruction, you rulers of the earth!
11 Serve Yahweh with fear
   and rejoice—with trembling.
12 Kiss the Son, lest he become angry
   and you perish in your tracks,
   for his wrath ignites quickly.
   Oh, the joy of all who take refuge in him!

World View

2

Paul Tripp tells of a birthday party for one of the little girls in a kindergarten class he was once teaching. The girl's mother had decorated the room, provided favors, and so on, but one kindergarten boy—jealous because the gifts and main attention were not his—was well on his way to making an obnoxious nuisance of himself and a near disaster of the party. Then one of the mothers walked over and knelt down beside this lad, turned his chair so that he had to look directly into her eyes, and said, 'Johnny, it's not your party!' Funny how we can be so provincial (and sinful) that we can't see beyond our own nose and interests.

And Psalm 2 wants to correct this problem; it says to us, 'You need to get the big view of things.' That's why Psalm 2 is Psalm 2, just as in our previous message we noted why Psalm 1 was Psalm 1. The position of these two psalms at the beginning of the Psalter is deliberate. Psalm 1 deals with the most urgent individual matter; you must know where you are going and must be sure you belong to the congregation of the righteous. Psalm 2 says that you must know where history is going; you must see the whole show; you must understand that *the world has been promised to the Messiah*. So what do you see and hear in Psalm 2?

The world that hates

First, you see the world that hates (vv. 1–3). Here is a *hostile* world—nations rage, peoples plot, kings and rulers conspire against Yahweh and his Anointed King. Whether congresses or parliaments, whether democracies or dictatorships, the root attitude of nations and of the head knockers of this age is: 'We do not want this man to reign over us' (Luke 19:14). This is Psalm 1:1 to the second power and writ large; this is what it looks like when the counsel of the wicked and the way of sinners and the seat of scoffers goes international.

The early church tells us that the premier example of this rebellion occurred in the crucifixion of Messiah Jesus (Acts 4:23–31). The Jewish brass had threatened the apostles; they came back and reported it all to the gathered believers, who then gave themselves to prayer and quoted Psalm 2:1–2 in that prayer and filled in the blanks of the latest and foremost king and ruler—Herod and Pontius Pilate, 'along with the Gentiles and the peoples of Israel' (v. 27). And here the church declares that the hostile world Psalm 2 describes is also a *persecuting* world—'And now, Lord, look upon their threats...' (v. 29). The hostility and enmity directed at Jesus is also, willy-nilly, directed at his people. And so the Psalm implies the Messiah's people will pay a huge price for belonging to him. This enmity may vary in intensity from time to time, but on the whole history runs red with the blood of Messiah's members.

It was so when the Communists took over China in 1949. Brother Yun of the underground church relates that in his home area of Nanyang, believers were crucified on the walls of their churches for refusing to deny Christ; others were chained to horses or vehicles and dragged to their deaths; a pastor was hoisted by a rope and makeshift crane and then dropped to the ground when he would not renounce Christ—the first time didn't kill him, so they did it once more to finish him off. Such episodes clutter history's calendar and our current century is already awash in such brutality. It is, sadly, par for the course. Hatred for the Messiah spills over on Messiah's people.

Yet the psalmist implies that this rebellious world, this persecuting world, is nevertheless an *insane* world. That is the implication behind his fourfold, astonished 'Why?' in verses 1-2. That 'why' is the first word in the psalm and only occurs once, but it is intended to 'carry over' to the following clauses (hence my translation). He can hardly believe it! What suicidal nincompoops to be possessed of such livid rage toward the God who rules.

So what are we to make of this? Well, if you are going to get a 'world view,' you must start here. If you are going to get a right view of God's kingdom, you must first get an accurate view of the world. Whether its rage always shows up at full fury, this world nevertheless hates God, detests his Messiah, and despises Messiah's people. 'If the world hates you,' Jesus has told us, 'know that it has hated me before it hated you. If you were of the world, the world would love its own; but because you are not of the world, but I chose you out of the world, therefore the world hates you' (John 15:18–19, RSV). Let the realism of the Bible's view infect your mind; be sure you understand what you can expect.

The throne that consoles

Secondly, you can see here the throne that consoles (vv. 4–6). Right off you see the divine reaction to world-wide human rebellion: 'The One who sits in the heavens laughs! The Lord mocks at them!' (v. 4). You get the picture? God is not fazed! The mighty politicians, the dictators in their military fatigues, the terrorists with their bomb loads strapped to their backs—God is unimpressed. If you have imbibed a western sentimental view of God as the great soupy softie in the sky, then you will not understand this picture of verse 4. In fact, it will likely 'offend' you. But the psalm implies that nations may strut out their nuclear bombs— it only convulses the Almighty in laughter! To think that a few swaggering sovereigns could destroy God's kingdom with such trifles! After you hear the kings in verse 3, you need to see this picture of the laughing God in verse 4, in order to get re-focused on the truth.

Sinclair Ferguson (in his book *Deserted by God?*) mentions how the onset of anger may cause some symptoms of depression to disappear. He tells of a nineteenth century London physician, a certain Dr. Williams, who was sought out by patients suffering from mild depression. He sometimes referred them to a premier consultant living in Scotland. Patients making the several days' journey by coach arrived only to soon discover that no such doctor existed. They spent their return journey scheming how they would vent their spleen on Dr. Williams. They were furious—but no longer depressed! Something else held their attention.

That is the effect verse 4 should have on the faith-full psalm reader. You hear the scary bravado of verse 3, but then you re-focus with the view of the laughing King in verse 4.

And there is also divine action in contrast to human decision (vv. 5–6). You may see it best by hearing! Place the words of the rulers of this age in verse 3 side-by-side with the Yahweh's words in verse 6: 'But I [the pronoun is emphatic] have installed my king on Zion, my holy hill.' They say, 'Let us...' and Yahweh says, 'But I....' When he mentions 'my king' he is referring to the one called 'his anointed' in verse 2. (For the record, I do not think that he refers here to any conceivable king of David's line; I think this psalm has its eyes on the final, culminating king of that line, the Messiah par excellence). So he mocks their puny rebellion (v. 4) and he has already installed the King who will rule the world (vv. 5–6).

And yet there's a bit of a 'kicker' here, for there is a certain divine 'weakness' in the face of this united human power. Yahweh has installed his king 'on Zion, my holy hill.' Of course, he is speaking of his choice of his covenant king, David, and David's line of kings that culminates in the Messiah himself. But look where he begins! The first reference in the Bible to Zion is in 2 Samuel 5:7, the stronghold of Zion that David took from the Jebusites. This 'Zion' was a puny 11 acres of real estate on the southeastern ridge of Jerusalem. Yahweh plants his kingdom there—and it will become a great mountain and fill the whole earth (Dan. 2:35). But he begins his visible kingdom in this world on a tiny, banana-shaped hill in a provincial backwater called Judah. God plants his kingdom in weakness, but because God plants it, it will prove undefeatable. It's a fascinating combination: weakness and invincibility.

And when God's servants are at their best they are aware of it. Australian missionary Dick McLellan has given us a case in point in his fascinating book, *Warriors of Ethiopia*. He tells of 42 evangelists from the Wolaitta tribe in southwestern Ethiopia who wanted to take the gospel to other tribes in the Gofa region. These men moved their families to Gofa, rented land, built houses, planted crops, had their new neighbors in, gossiped the gospel to them. Some of them received the Savior. Prayer houses were built where they met for fellowship and worship. But too many changes took place: converts no longer went to witchdoctors, no longer paid the priest's tax to the Orthodox priests, no longer slipped bribes to government officials for needs or favors. So...a police lieutenant arrested the evangelist Atero, chained his wrists together and clamped his ankles together in heavy iron rings so he could only hop but not walk. He paraded Atero in front of the market-day crowd and let it be known that this was what would happen to any who followed the 'new religion.' He ordered Atero, 'Go back to Wolaitta...and take your Jesus thing with you! We don't want your Jesus here!' Then McLellan says that Atero hopped forward and said: 'O Sir, listen. Please listen. I can go but the Gospel will stay. By the power of God I planted Jesus in Gofa. He is planted in the hearts and souls of the Gofa people. I can go but Jesus will stay.' As if Atero says to one of the 'rulers of this age', 'There are some things you can change but some that you can't—some are irreversible, even for those with power.' I planted Jesus in Gofa. I can go but Jesus will stay! And God's kingdom may look pretty flimsy, planted in little Zion. But God has planted his kingdom there and that will stay—and no one can do anything about it.

So you live in a world that hates. But you lift your eyes and see the throne that consoles. I rather like the way the Jerusalem Bible translates verse 4a: 'The One whose throne is in heaven sits laughing.' It's the same message as in Revelation 4: there is a throne—and One who is sitting upon it. Keep your eyes there. Sometimes that's all that will keep you sane.

The decree that determines

Thirdly, you need to hear the decree that determines (vv. 7–9). I also need to explain a detail of the text in verse 7. Most English translations refer to the 'decree of Yahweh/the LORD.' However, the accents in the traditional Hebrew text indicate that 'Yahweh' is the emphatic subject of the verb 'said.' So…we have another speaker beginning in verse 7; he is going to tell us about the 'decree.' It was Yahweh himself who spoke this decree to 'me.' The 'me' is the anointed king, the Messiah.

There are three keynotes in this decree about the Messiah's reign. The first is *legitimacy*: 'You are my son; I have begotten you this very day' (7b). Yahweh has appointed him to rule and has installed him (I believe that 'begotten' in v. 7 is equivalent to 'installed' in v. 6). He is the rightful king. Then there is the *scope* of his rule in verse 8 ('nations…ends of the earth')—his will be an international, world-wide kingdom. It is all to belong to Jesus. And then he indicates the *force* of his rule in verse 9: 'You will break them with an iron rod, you will smash them to pieces like a clay pot.'

Why, we might think, I was just beginning to warm to Christ's kingdom and then, suddenly, it turns vicious. But you must understand verse 9 in light of verse 3. When the time comes to fully enforce his kingly rule, Christ will not be welcomed with open arms. He comes to a God-hating, Christ-defying world. The kingdom of our Lord and of his Christ does not come because the world welcomes his reign and evolves into the kingdom of God, but it comes because Christ imposes his reign by force on rebellious people. So get the picture the decree gives you: The appointed King (v. 7) with world-wide sway (v. 8) to be established in overwhelming force (v. 9). That is the decree that is controlling history.

Marvin Olasky tells of the latter years of newspaper tycoon William Randolph Hearst. His house guests had to abide by a strict rule: 'Never mention death in Mr Hearst's presence.' That may have been harder than you think. One can forget oneself when talk is flowing (if it ever did there). You would have to walk on conversational eggshells, pretending you were at a convention of Christian Scientists! But that was the 'decree'—and it controlled life and talk apparently in the Hearst household.

And in this psalm, Yahweh's decree controls history. The will of God for Jesus' life is in verses 7b–9. This is the word that determines what will take place and prevail in the history of this world. The certainty of this decree needs to infect your world and life view. It should color the way you look at politics and world conditions. You may not know what to make of them always—but you know where history is headed; you know what the decree is and how it will control and shape everything. It's what keeps God's people glued together during the present age.

The gospel that calls

Finally, you must hear the gospel that calls (vv. 10–12). Here it is as if the psalmist himself speaks but clearly it is the Lord's invitation. God is so utterly unguessable! He addresses kings and rulers—apparently the very same kings and rulers described in verse 2! They are given an opportunity for mercy. The rebels are called to make the only reasonable response (vv. 10–12a). There are two incentives: there is a danger to avoid (lest the Son become angry and you perish in your tracks, 12b) and a joy to experience (12c). The New Berkley Version has nicely captured this latter note and I have 'cobbed' its rendering: 'Oh, the joy of all who take refuge in him.' Both danger and delight are held out to move them to repentance.

So what must they do? 'Serve Yahweh.' That is, become slaves of Yahweh. Not especially an appealing option to kings and rulers. And they are to 'kiss the Son,' Yahweh's appointed Messiah. I don't think the Hebrew text is as difficult here as some of our translations pretend and I don't think we need to have allergies over the fact that the word for 'son' here is Aramaic instead of Hebrew. The kiss is the sign of submission. When a near eastern king reported the subjugation and homage of a conquered king he would say 'what's-his-name, king-of-wherever, came and kissed my feet.' And even we rebels who run around without a crown on our heads face the same demand (and opportunity): give your total submission to the Son.

The symbolism may vary, the reality remains. I mentioned Dick McLellan earlier. He tells of a witch-doctor named Onisa and a slave called Gebre who arrived at his missions home wanting to know if he—McLellan—was Jesus. They had heard a garbled mix of rumor and error and arrived with their questions at a time when terrific storms had done much damage to homes in that area of Ethiopia. But a native evangelist arrived at McLellan's place and so missionary and evangelist spent two days and most of three nights making clear the gospel story and the truth about Jesus to these two seekers. Onisa and Gebre both believed and came to faith in Christ. To acknowledge and confess that faith they stood before a small group of believers. Then they held their right hands high and renounced Satan, blood sacrifices, evil practices and all their sin. Then, McLellan reports, they raised both hands high and said, 'Having renounced Satan and believing in my heart that Jesus is the Son of God Who died for me, I take Him as my Saviour with two hands. I will never deny Him.' To give both hands was a sign of complete surrender. It's the same as to kiss the Son. And that is Yahweh's kingdom word to you today: Kiss the Son, take his Messiah-king with two hands.

PSALM 3

A psalm of David; when he fled from Absalom his son.

1 Yahweh, how many are my foes!
   How many are rising up against me!
2 How many are saying about me,
   'There's no salvation for him in God.' [Selah.]

3 But **you**, Yahweh, are a shield around me,
   my glory, and the one who lifts up my head.
4 With my voice I cry out to Yahweh,
   and he answered me from his holy hill. [Selah.]

5 **I** have lain down and gone off to sleep;
   I woke up again, for **Yahweh** sustains me.
6 I will not be afraid of ten thousands of people
   who have set themselves all around me.

7 Rise, Yahweh! Save me, my God!
   for you shall strike all my enemies on the jaw,
   you shall shatter the teeth of the wicked.
8 Salvation is Yahweh's doing;
   upon your people (be) your blessing. [Selah.]

Thick Trouble

There's an entry in Kenneth MacRae's diary in July of 1913 in which he alludes to 'that godly man Peter MacDonald,' who confessed to wondering if he had ever really prayed in his life. We may wonder the same when we meet with these prayers in the Psalms. What am I, spiritual pigmy that I am, doing wandering around among these mighty prayers?

Of course there are always debunkers. Arm-chair types who allege that prayer is simply believers' form of escapism, of failing to deal with life as it really is—whatever that means. We've no time for those who insinuate that prayer is an anemic exercise engaged in by pale, pasty-looking creatures who have trouble coping with challenges. Bible Christians know better. It's as clear as the title to Psalm 3: 'when he fled from Absalom his son.' Prayer is the way we slug our way through troubles. To paraphrase Eugene Peterson (in *Answering God*), trouble triggers prayer.

The background to the psalm then is Absalom's rebellion in 2 Samuel 15–18, when David's son tried to seize David's kingship by snuffing out David's life and loyalists. All this was part of Yahweh's judgment on David's Bathsheba-Uriah fiasco (see 2 Sam. 12:10–12). But there's another angle we dare not forget. In his lust for the crown Absalom was trying to unseat the king Yahweh had installed on his holy hill (Ps. 2:6). Absalom had joined the ranks of the international scoundrels of Psalm 2:1–3 in their plot to overthrow Yahweh's chosen king. And this thick trouble drives Yahweh's king to prayer.

One more 'intro' note. Isn't the placing of Psalm 3 interesting? You first go through the double doors of the Psalter—Psalm 1 tells you to settle your commitment and Psalm 2 to get a clear view of the kingdom. Then what? You walk into trouble (Psalm 3). In fact, there's so much trouble in these following psalms that—as Geoffrey Grogan points out in *Prayer, Praise & Prophecy*—not many readers are able to wade through the first 'book' of the Psalms without giving out.

So here is David's prayer in trouble. Maybe it's a prayer for you. Let's walk through it, remembering David is the special king but allowing you to nevertheless identify with him.

The enemies you face

First, then, there are the enemies you face (vv. 1–2). 'How many...how many...how many...'—nothing but enemies, lots of them. They are many, mean, and mouthy. And it's especially their *words* that grate. 'There's no salvation for him in God.' By that they don't mean that God cannot help David but that he will not help him (cf. Matt. 27:43). Such words can stir up an especially gut-wrenching temptation, for their words—whether said of David or me—are in one sense all too true: I don't deserve the least of God's mercies. The best defense is simply to admit the fact.

Patrick Kavanaugh tells how a friend of George Frideric Handel in all innocence told the composer about how dreary some of the music was that he had heard at the Vauxhall Gardens. Handel simply replied, 'You are right, sir, it is pretty poor stuff. I thought so myself when I wrote it.' That draws the sting; then one can get on to the real problem.

But verse 2 shows us how subtle our despair may be; it may come more from the enemies' words than from their weapons, more from their suggestion than from their attack as such. What then does one do? What did David do? Well, what is he doing in verses 1–2? He is telling Yahweh about it. The very God, who, his enemies say, wants nothing to do with him, is the One to whom he cries. And what do you tell Yahweh in such a case? You tell him that many are saying that He wants no truck with you—you pour your anguish at the feet of a God who is not supposed to care.

The God you confess

Now the focus falls upon the God you confess (vv. 3–4). Here is the turning-point: after the repeated 'how-manys' he does a grammatical '180' and fills his vision with his God. 'But you [emphatic], Yahweh…'

What sort of God does he have? (1) A protecting God; you are 'a shield around me.' Precisely the sort of God David desperately needed in the Absalom peril of 2 Samuel 15–18. (2) A sufficient God; David calls Yahweh 'my glory,' a term that connotes the ideas of weightiness, substance, wealth. His kingdom is taken from him, but

Yahweh is his glory (Franz Delitzsch). That is, he is losing his 'glory' (apparently to Absalom) and yet he has all the 'glory' he needs in Yahweh himself.

Let me digress momentarily to suggest that there could be a bit more packed into this use of 'glory.' You may remember those episodes of Israel's 'rebellion in the wilderness' in the book of Numbers. Whether it's a chunk of Israel or Korah & Co. who are ready to lay into Moses and Aaron—just when they are ready to do so 'the glory of Yahweh' appears (Num. 14:10; 16:19, 42). The glory-cloud of Yahweh's blazing presence appears at precisely the needed time to defend his servants. In Numbers 14 and 16 the 'glory' of Yahweh speaks of his readiness to intervene in order to defend a leader who is under assault. I cannot be sure David had this context in mind when he speaks of Yahweh as 'my glory'—but it would certainly fit his context and comfort his soul. If so, then 'my glory' suggests that Yahweh is both a sufficient and a defending God.

So Yahweh is a protecting, sufficient, and (3) a restoring God—David calls him 'the one who lifts up my head.' One finds the idea in Genesis 40:13, 20–21, when Pharaoh

What kind of God is Yahweh?

• protecting
• sufficient
• restoring
• accessible

'lifts up the head' of his cupbearer and restores him to his office (though there was a different head-lifting for the chief baker!). During Absalom's revolt, David was in dire need of Yahweh's restoring touch (2 Sam. 15:30). Then David implies that Yahweh is (4) an accessible God: 'With my voice I cry out to Yahweh, and he answered me from his holy hill.' Vocal, desperate prayer. What's fascinating about this is that David is leaving Jerusalem, leaving the site of the tabernacle, putting geography between himself and the 'holy hill.' But his prayers get to Yahweh's 'holy hill' even when David has no physical access there. In a mere two verses and four lines of poetry David fills his vision with the character of his God.

In *Flags of Our Fathers*, James Bradley tells of the famous photograph of the Marines raising the American flag on Iwo Jima in 1945. It appeared in numerous papers, including a hometown Texas newspaper being perused by Ed Block, home on leave from the Air Force. His mother Belle walked by, glanced at the photograph, pointed to the marine thrusting the pole down in the ground and told Ed that was his brother Harlon. Ed refuted his mother: there was no side view, just the back of a marine; besides they didn't even know if Harlon was on Iwo Jima; there's no way she could know that that fellow was her Harlon. But Belle was sure; as she strode into the kitchen she simply said, 'I know my boy.' Actually, that figure was identified as Henry Hansen. But Belle Block was still unmoved. Sadly, the family soon received word that Harlon had been killed in action on Iwo Jima. But in 1947, after additional testimony, they received notification of a correction: Henry Hansen had not been in the picture; the lad aiming the pole into the ground was Harlon Block. Belle Block was hardly surprised: 'I know my boy.'

That is the sort of thing David is saying in verses 3–4. In the middle of his mess he is saying, 'I know my God.' In face of the threats and ruckus and theological opinions of his enemies David turns his eyes to his protecting, sufficient, restoring, accessible God. The God-centeredness of his gaze keeps him steady while his enemies try to decide what precise level of scum he is.

The peace you enjoy

In view of this, you can think, thirdly, of the peace you enjoy (vv. 5–6).

'I have lain down and gone off to sleep.' What on earth is David doing, you might ask, going off to sleep when there's a coup afoot? The sequence of the text explains it: The emphatic 'I' of verse 5 comes after the emphatic 'But you' of verse 3. Because you, O Lord, are what you are, I can go take a snooze. Alec Motyer (in his *Treasures of the King*) nicely captures the stress of the text: 'The subject ("I") is emphatic—just imagine this being true of me! Placed as I am!—and the verbs are past tense, looking back on a delightful, if surprising, experience: "For my part, I went to bed, and how I slept! I woke up, for Yahweh himself keeps sustaining me."'

Note that this peace is both immediate (v. 5) and long-term (v. 6); it covers both the first night (v. 5) and the unforeseeable future (v. 6). David, however, takes nothing for granted; he explains why he awoke—'for Yahweh sustains me.' Is that not always the explanation of bed-sleep-waking? But David is not held in the grip of fear, for this peace is not a one-night flash but (as v. 6 shows) controls the way he looks at the future with all its uncertainty.

We dare not pontificate on all situations, but verse 5 implies that *your peace may be immediate*. The definitive relief had not yet come. David does not have peace from turmoil but peace in it. What did David do that night as Absalom plotted his ruin? Went to sleep. No Tylenol PM. Sometimes God works that way.

Irene Howat (*Finding God Is in the Darkness*) tells of the heart-wrenching trial of Pat and Andrew Cardy in 1981. They lived in Northern Ireland; their nine-year-old Jennifer had cycled off to a friend's house to play—and never came back. A week later she was found; murdered. What days and nights those were while they were waiting and searching and not knowing for sure. Probably about the fourth day, Pat's doctor dropped off some sleeping tablets for her, and that night she took herself to bed with her tablets, wondering if they were to be her constant crutch. Before bed she was meditating and soon the words of a verse came to mind: 'It is vain for you to rise up early, to sit up late, to eat the bread of sorrows, for so he giveth his beloved sleep' (Ps. 127:2, KJV). As she thought on those words and on the love in which they were wrapped, she claimed them, and slept peacefully that night—and every night afterwards. It didn't bring Jennifer back; it didn't bring a magical end to her anguish. But sometimes Yahweh does that—he gives peace in trouble and tragedy, and may do so immediately.

David would understand. He goes off to sleep. Yahweh can look after his own kingdom. He didn't have any Sominex—only a God who shields and sustains. No circumstances have yet changed, and yet there is no alarm or anxiety.

The help you expect

Finally, in verses 7–8 you come to the help you expect. Right away I will mention that you'll find the verbs in verse 7 handled differently in various translations. There are about five different ways one can construe these verbs and we can't suck up space to explain it all here. So let me simply explain how I am taking them...

There is a certain tension in verse 7. When David cries, 'Rise, Yahweh! Save me, my God!' (7a), we can see that deliverance has *not yet* actually come. He has peace (vv. 5–6), but Absalom & Co. are still on the loose, wanting to spill his blood and pilfer his kingdom. And yet he is sure of deliverance. I've translated the verbs of verse 7b as futures. However, these Hebrew verbs are really what Anglos would call 'past' tenses. I think this is what David is doing: he is so certain of rescue that he describes it as already having taken place (past), even though, strictly speaking, it is yet future (hence my translation).

But this leads to a problem. There are some who always get upset when we get into parts of a psalm like this. Notice the violent imagery of verse 7b: 'for you shall strike all my enemies on the jaw, you shall shatter the teeth of the wicked.' Some get bent out of shape because the enemies are going to need an orthodontist. These people are nervous because this prayer asks God to get violent. Remember the hymn some churches sing: 'For not with swords loud clashing, nor roll of stirring drums; with deeds of love and mercy the heavenly kingdom comes.' Shall we pass the hand cream? And some are disturbed because David seems so vengeful—another woeful example of those crude Old Testament saints, they say. But he's not vengeful—clearly, in this prayer, he is committing vengeance to God and asking him for deliverance. But you must understand something here: if David is going to be 'saved' in this situation, then God will have to bring down those who oppose his chosen king. There can be no safety for David unless his enemies are eliminated.

Some months ago I ran across a clip in WORLD magazine about Bessy. Bessy is/was a Burmese python that accidentally was set loose in an Idaho apartment complex. A posse of plumbers was called in to find the 8-foot reptile among the walls and pipes of the 57,000-square-foot complex. They found Bessy loitering in the ceiling in the apartment below her proper 'home.' For two weeks residents had been nervously checking beneath beds and under sheets for the huge snake. After hearing the news of Bessy's discovery one resident confessed, 'We'll definitely sleep better.' No mystery there. Until the threat is removed, it's hard to feel secure.

That is the way it is with David's situation. Only his enemies are worse than a pet python. For David to have 'salvation' his enemies must be destroyed. He can have no lasting security unless that is so. You find the same kind of thing in the New Testament. Look at that prayer of the martyrs in Revelation 6:9-10—it is not a nice prayer but recognizes that if God's servants are to ever be vindicated those who crush them must be liquidated and judged. All this to say that, biblically, *salvation' can be a nasty piece of work.*

But let's note what David is wanting here when he asks for God to 'save' him (v. 7a) and confesses that 'salvation' is Yahweh's forte (v. 8). The salvation David speaks of here is a broad sort of thing—it includes deliverance from the clutches of Absalom. So salvation in this text is not limited to what we sometimes mean by it when we use it as almost synonymous with justification or entering the kingdom of God. Here it clearly included physical deliverance, the way God repeatedly acts for us in the crises and nasty times of life. We should not make too much of this, but neither should we make too little of it.

I remember my week at Bible camp when I was ten or twelve years old. The counselor for our cabin was 'Uncle Amos,' a minister who was spending his week at camp caring for his bunch of 'boys.' After lights were out one night and we were all in our bunks, we were talking there in the dark. Uncle Amos was inquiring of us whether we had been 'saved.' One of the lads answered that Jesus had saved him, because one time he and a friend were walking down the side of the road and a driver careened off the road into the ditch but didn't hit the two boys. Jesus had surely 'saved' him. Now I wasn't very brilliant but I do remember thinking to myself, 'That's not what Uncle Amos wants to hear! He means something much different by "saved"!' I'm sure I was right about Uncle Amos, but that kid may have known more about salvation than I! There is a sense in which Yahweh saves you again and again in your troubles and dangers. Some of you can point to having been 'saved' in that sense even this last week. We shouldn't forget this sense of 'salvation.' Maybe some of us are in arrears in the gratitude department if we haven't been remembering this.

'Upon your people (be) your blessing.' The psalm ends with a benediction. It's as if David said, 'Lord, it's not just my emergency, my fear, my enemies—but these situations are the lot of your people; let your blessing, your saving help also flow to them in their troubles.' And isn't David 'spot on'? Aren't there any number of you who come dragging your anxieties and your troubles into these pews and up to the Lord's table because you want to talk with Jesus about them?

PSALM 4

For the music leader. With stringed instruments.
A psalm of David.

1 Answer me when I call, O God of my righteousness.
   In tight places you have made space for me.
   Show grace to me and hear my prayer.

2 Sons of men,
        how long will my glory become mockery?
        how long will you love emptiness?
        how long will you seek lies? [Selah.]

3 But know that Yahweh has set apart the covenant one
        for himself;
   Yahweh will hear when I call to him.

4 Be angry but do not sin:
   Speak in your hearts upon your beds
        and keep quiet.[Selah.]

5 Sacrifice right sacrifices
   and trust yourselves to Yahweh.

6 Many keep saying, 'Who will show us good?'
   Lift up upon us the light of your face, O Yahweh!

7 You have placed more gladness in my heart
        than when their grain and new wine overflows.

8 In peace I will both lie down and go off to sleep,
        for you alone, Yahweh, will make me dwell securely.

Evening Prayer

4

It doesn't take much to turn your circumstances sour. You may be running out of your office building to catch lunch with a friend and—just before you step into your vehicle—realize that you've stepped in a wad of bubble gum that some under-motivated person couldn't bring themselves to dispose of properly. The psalms don't deal in such relative trivia but the sudden turn-around in circumstances is the same. You go through Psalms 1 and 2 with the assurance that the Lord knows the way of the righteous and that the world has been given to the Messiah to rule only to have the world fall apart. The heading of Psalm 3 and the content of Psalm 4 make this clear. We don't know if the trouble in Psalm 4 is the same as in Psalm 3 (Absalom's rebellion). Some expositors believe that it is. In any case, the two psalms can be taken as a pair, since Psalm 3 seems to be a morning prayer (v. 5 there) and Psalm 4 an evening prayer (vv. 4, 8). Whatever the trouble, Psalm 4 shows it is *valuable* trouble, for the heading shows that this psalm came to be used in public worship. This is a prayer that seems intent on correcting our thinking, directing our discipleship, and increasing our faith. So what do we find in this evening prayer?

Urgency and Confidence

We find, first, urgency and confidence in prayer (v. 1). Clearly, David knows God's character—he calls him 'God of my righteousness,' that is, he is the God who will show me to be in the right, even though I am misjudged and persecuted. We would likely put our experience first but the psalmist puts God's character first in his prayer.

That gives him confidence, and so does the fact that he has experienced God's help: 'in tight places you have made space for me.' The verb is past tense—God has already done this for David. The word for 'tight places' carries the idea of being pressed or squeezed, but the Lord brings relief by 'making space' in such conditions. 'You have given me relief when I was in distress' (ESV) conveys the same idea.

All of this leads him to expect God's grace: 'show grace to me and hear my prayer.' His plea for grace implies a lack of resources; he is in a desperate and helpless condition. Yet he is not in despair but has confidence that Yahweh will hear him because of Yahweh's character and previous help received. In the first lines of his prayer David declares God's character, remembers God's mercies, and presses his emergency; he focuses on God's tendencies, remembers God's goodness, then pleads for God's grace. *Biblical prayer seems to ponder God a good deal more than we are prone to do.*

What is the import of this initial snip of David's prayer for us? Well, note how he combines thoughtfulness (God's character and help) and urgency (God's grace for his need). The two go together. When our youngest son was very small he used to cause both his grandfathers some emotional angst because he did not use milk on his cereal. One of them would see Joel eating his breakfast cereal dry and simply could not understand why he did—or how he could do— that. And, of course, they were right. There is something mildly gastronomically repulsive about eating cereal without milk; it should be cereal *and* milk. So David's prayer: thoughtfulness and urgency. Prayer is not merely a technique for maintaining emotional equilibrium. Prayer is worship that is both intelligent and desperate.

Warning and Counsel

Secondly, we find in this prayer warning and counsel in teaching (vv. 2–6). David not only prays but in his prayer talks to and teaches people. He seems to address various groups.

He speaks to the *slanderers* (vv. 2–3). They bring empty charges against David with no basis in fact and spread lies about the king (NIV is too interpretive in 2b). What defense or recourse does he have? He has Yahweh's special attention and regard: 'know that Yahweh has set apart the covenant one for himself.' Here the 'covenant one' refers to David himself as king. It is my attempt to render the word *hasid* (some translate 'godly'). You can detect that it seems related to *hesed*, unfailing love. So there is sometimes a debate—does *hasid* refer to one who has *received* Yahweh's *hesed* or to someone who *shows* it? Alec Motyer cuts through the problem: the *hasid* is the one loved by God and who loves him back. Here David seems especially conscious as the covenant one/*ḥasîd* that he has received Yahweh's unfailing love in what we call the Davidic covenant (cf. 2 Sam. 22:51). And because he is covenant king Yahweh has placed him under special protection: he has 'set [him] apart.' This verb (*pālâ*) appears in Exodus 8:22, 9:4, and 11:7 when Yahweh 'makes a distinction' between Israel and the Egyptians—Israel would not be plagued by flies, nor would their cattle or first-born be destroyed; they are given special protection during a time of danger and attack on others. So here David senses he stands under the special protection of Yahweh—and has the peculiar privilege of access to Yahweh ('Yahweh will hear when I call to him').

Now David was a covenant one in a premier sense; as the covenant king we could say he stands a cut above Joe-Schmoe Christian. But this should prove no discouragement, for in principle we still stand in David's sandals. He shows us here that *the weapon against slander is to remember how God regards you, to hold on to what he has said about you.* And we may not be covenant kings, but if we are uncondemned, chosen, prayed for, and loved (Rom. 8:33–5), it doesn't sound too second-class. If Yahweh has said to us, 'Don't be afraid, for I have redeemed you; I have called you by name—you are mine' (Isa. 43:1), why should we listen to the blabberings of our enemies, or even the accusations of an overly-sensitive conscience?

Paul Boller tells of the time Thomas Jefferson went into a Baltimore hotel to ask for accommodation. He was in his working clothes, apparently a bit splattered with mud, and the proprietor, giving him the once-over, retorted, 'We have no room for you, sir.' Jefferson repeated his request, and when it was denied once more, called for his horse and left to find a more congenial reception somewhere. A friend soon came in and told the proprietor that the man who had just left was Thomas Jefferson, the Vice President of the United States. Anguish and remorse! He had thought he was dealing with a dirty farmer. But because someone thought Jefferson was a dirty farmer didn't change the fact that he was Vice President. Those who despise us may regard us as a step above scum but that does not alter the fact that we are covenant ones whom Yahweh has set apart for himself.

Next, David speaks to the *angry* (vv. 4–5). The plural, imperative verbs continue, but the addressees seem to have changed. Now he seems to be speaking to some group who are associates but who are 'stewed' over the injustice and wrong of the situation. They are hotheads, probably some of his supporters, who were pro-king, pro-David, but ticked off at what was going on (cf. Ps. 37:1, 7–8). I have retained the traditional translation 'be angry' for the first verb in verse 4. It is a verb (*rāgaz*) that means to tremble, shake, or quake, and either fear or anger may cause the trembling (cf. Gen. 45:24; 2 Kings 19:27, 28; Job 12:6; Prov. 29:9; and Ezek. 16:43, where anger or rage seem involved). Of course, Paul picks up this text in Ephesians 4:26. But our concern is with this psalm.

So I take it that David says, 'Be angry and do not sin.' Now how do you do that? Primarily by focusing on the last verb of verse 4, 'keep quiet.' The way you can be angry and not sin is by keeping your thoughts to yourself ('speak in your hearts upon your beds') and by keeping your mouth shut ('and keep quiet'). That is the immediate response needed. Verse 5 lays down the ongoing positive activities:

offering right sacrifices, which involves atonement for sin, and trusting themselves and their case to Yahweh. But that immediate response of verse 4b is crucial.

Harry Truman took on a heavy load when he became president of the United States in 1945 after Franklin Roosevelt's death. He was so plunged into his work that he was inadvertently neglecting his wife. Harry arrived home in Independence, Missouri, to spend Christmas with his family and stepped into a marital meatgrinder. According to Paul Boller (*Presidential Wives*), Bess Truman met him with: 'I guess you couldn't think of any more reasons to stay away. As far as I'm concerned, you might as well have stayed in Washington.' It went downhill from there. A big fight. When Truman returned to Washington on December 27, he was still so hot he wrote Bess a simmering letter and mailed it by special delivery that very night. The next morning he was on the phone to his daughter Margaret— with instructions: go to the post office; talk to Edgar Hinde the postmaster; tell him to give you a special delivery letter addressed to your mother; it's an angry letter; I don't want her to see it; so burn it.

'Speak in your hearts upon your beds and keep quiet.' The teaching is not advocating repression; it is not denying anger or rage, but acknowledging the need to control it in a proper and godly fashion. One of the godliest things you can do when you are irate about unjust suffering is to keep your mouth shut. This teaching runs counter to the fad in some 'Christian' circles that says you have the right to nourish, feed, and stir your anger and resentment—you even have the right to be angry at God. Of course, we would have to be omniscient to be rightly angry at God.

Then David turns to the *despairing* (v. 6). We have both a prevalent (note: *many* are saying) and a persisting (the verb form is a participle: *keep on* saying) attitude here. I take their words to be limited to the question of 6a: 'Who will show us good?' They are in the pit of discouragement. We can't deny this is how we tend to react. Sometimes we may do it vicariously, when the trouble does not directly involve us. Here is someone in our congregation—we've earnestly been praying for them and yet more and more troubles come over them. Or sometimes it seems like trouble is contagious, and we can think of two dozen people in a congregation who've been hit with disease or disaster or difficulty. And in our despondency we ask when God will reverse the rising slop-level of life.

What does David say to this? He lifts a line out of the worship service. He paraphrases part of the benediction the priests pronounced over Israel in the tabernacle worship (see Num. 6:24–6): 'Lift up upon us the light of your face, O Yahweh!' (v. 6b). He takes the priests' benediction and turns it into a prayer—for Yahweh's favor upon the despairing. Apparently, David actually believes that benediction. For him it's not a mere ditty at the end of worship, not a bunch of religious frosting or a snazzy way of saying 'the end.' Interesting, isn't it, that sometimes what you need for the next step is right there in the worship service? If nothing more, this verse shows us *the lively concern we ought to have for those among us who are overwhelmed.*

So that is the teaching in this psalm; warning and counsel to the slanderers, the angry, and the despairing.

Joy and Peace

Lastly, we meet with joy and peace in believing (vv. 7–8). Here David is addressing Yahweh directly again. He revels in *massive joy* (v 7). This joy is divine ('you have placed'), internal ('in my heart'), abundant ('more gladness than...'), and independent. I say 'independent' because he implies that 'their' gladness is dependent and based solely on their circumstances (when their grain and wine overflow). Their gladness comes because their income tax return has been finished or their indigestion is cured or their harvest immense. Note that it is an *Old Testament believer* who says this—as if he is saying to you that Romans 15:13 is really true! He has a gladness in the midst of trouble, a gladness that trouble cannot destroy or snuff out.

And then he says he enjoys *deep peace* (v. 8). This peace is secure, because Yahweh protects it (v. 8b), and tangible, because with it he can go off to sleep (v. 8a). 'In peace I will both lie down and go off to sleep, for you alone, Yahweh, will make me dwell securely.' Graham Scroggie has referred to that October night in 1555 that was to be Nicolas Ridley's last on earth. The next day Oxford would see him burning at the stake for his faith. But on that night before Ridley's execution his brother offered to stay with him in his last hours. But the bishop refused, saying that he meant to go to bed and sleep as quietly as he ever did in his life. Understandably so; if it's going to be one's last night on earth, why wreck it all by not getting a decent night's sleep? 'In *peace* I will both lie down and go off to sleep, for you alone, Yahweh, will make me to dwell securely.' Don't think this is unusually heroic or utterly unreal; it's just what happens to helpless believers who throw themselves upon the God who keeps them.

PSALM 5

For the music leader. To nehiloth. A psalm of David.

1 Give ear to my words, O Yahweh,
   understand my murmuring.
2 Pay attention to the voice of my cry for help,
   my King and my God,
   for it is to **you** that I pray.
3 O Yahweh, in the morning you will hear my voice,
   in the morning I will set in order (my requests) to you
   and watch expectantly.

4 For you are not a God who delights in wickedness;
   evil can never be a guest of yours.
5 Arrogant men will never hold their ground in your presence;
   you hate all evildoers.
6 You cause those who speak lies to perish;
   Yahweh detests bloodthirsty and deceitful men.

7 But **I**, in your overflowing and faithful love,
    will enter your house;
  I will bow down toward your holy temple in the fear of you.
8 Yahweh, lead me in your righteousness
    because of those lurking for me;
  make your way straight before me.
9 For there is nothing reliable in their mouths,
  their heart is destruction,
  their throat is an open grave;
  with their tongues they speak smooth talk.

10 Hold them guilty, O God!
  Let them fall because of their schemes;
  banish them for their many rebellious deeds,
  for they have revolted against you.
11 But let all who take refuge in you rejoice,
  let them shout for joy forever;
  and may you be their shelter,
  and may those who love your name exult in you!
12 For **you** will bless the righteous one, Yahweh;
  you will wrap him round with favor like a shield.

Prayer Tutorial

5

Moody Stuart once asked John ('Rabbi') Duncan to preach for him. Rabbi Duncan replied, 'I'll be glad to preach, if you'll take the prayers; I'm not able to pray at present, but I can preach a bit, and would like it.' We may be unsure how to take Rabbi Duncan. He assumed preaching was easier than praying (I think he's right). I don't know what was behind his 'not (being) able to pray.' But his attitude is far ahead of one that assumes all one needs is a reservoir of pious lingo and turns of phrase. The best posture for praying is to realize that we need help for praying. We begin prayer by praying, 'Lord, teach us to pray' (Luke 11:1), and mature believers find themselves praying that petition again and again. And I have a suspicion that in the Holy Spirit's filing cabinet there is a folder marked 'instruction in prayer' and inside, among others, is a copy of Psalm 5. In this psalm David teaches us how to pray when we are in dangerous and lousy circumstances. In his own prayer he models prayer for us and provides us with a prayer tutorial, so that, as he himself prays, he seems to leave behind directions for our prayers. Let's look at these.

Prepare your prayer

First he says: prepare your prayer (vv. 1–3). Note that David does not pray to a distant stranger. He is speaking to Yahweh, 'my King and my God' (v. 2). Yahweh is the redeeming God who is there for his people (Exod. 3:1–15) and he has brought David into a personal bond with himself. On this basis prayer can begin.

Note how he describes his prayer. It consists of spoken words ('my words,' 1a) but also of broken words ('my murmuring,' 1b). 'Murmuring' may mean groaning or sighing; in Psalm 39:3 it seems to indicate a disturbed sort of 'musing' that is non-verbal. The murmuring here may be like that—distraught concerns that cannot be formulated in words—and he asks Yahweh to 'understand' it! As if he already knows a Romans 8:26 kind of God! And he comes with desperate words, for he speaks of 'the voice of my cry for help' (2a). His prayer is not calm and sedate but is driven by the urgency of his dangerous situation.

Yet for all this tension he comes with prepared words: 'in the morning I will set in order my requests.' The verb means to set out in order, to arrange, to set in rows. It is used in Leviticus 1:7–8, of the priests arranging the wood on the altar fire and arranging the chunks of the sacrificial animal on the altar; it is used of arranging the showbread in two rows of six loaves each on the tabernacle table (Lev. 24:8). It's an orderly verb! It does not have an explicit object here in verse 3, but I think David is thinking of his prayer, his requests. The priests may be setting the morning sacrifice in order but David is getting together and ordering his prayer. He is *preparing* his prayer.

We find too little of this in the church. We don't order our prayers; we simply start in with our religious rattling and easy Christian clichés. 'We just want to thank you, Lord; we're just really glad to be here; we ask you, Lord, to just give us a really good time in your presence; just help us to worship you in Spirit and in truth [How many ponder what that means in John 4? Has it perhaps become an empty phrase that simply makes excellent 'filler'?] tonight and we'll be careful to give you all the honor and glory... blah, blah, blah.' Then if we need to pad the prayer or to boost its 'earnestness,' we can always insert 'Father' or 'Lord' every third or fourth word—go ahead; surely God's not too interested in our keeping the third commandment anymore. I suppose some might call this 'free prayer.' It's certainly free, I doubt if it's prayer. Sometimes we may need to revert to using the written prayers of others to get back on track. Like praying the psalms themselves as our prayers. Or using the *Book of Common Prayer* (gulp for some) or the Puritan prayers collected in *The Valley of Vision* or chunks out of Matthew Henry's *Method for Prayer*. There is a difference between prayer and drivel. I do not want to advocate eloquence in prayer, but I want to reject thoughtlessness in prayer. 'In the morning I will set in order my requests to you.' Prepare your prayer.

Know your God

David seems to give a second direction: know your God (vv. 4–6). Be sure to note the connection in the first of verse 4, '*For* you are not...' The NIV exasperatingly omits the 'For.' But it is important. These verses are giving the reason or supplying the basis for David's expectancy in verses 1–3. Why is David watching expectantly (3c)? Because ('For,' 4a) he knows what God is like; he knows his character.

But what a character God is! He is not a God who delights in wickedness (4a); evil can never be a house guest of God's (4b); arrogant men will not stand in his presence (5a). Well, yes; that's probably the way we want a holy God to be. But it gets more surprising; at least David seems a bit shocking to a sentimentalized twenty-first century mind-set: Yahweh hates all evildoers; will cause those who speak lies to perish; and detests bloodthirsty and deceitful men (5b–6). No tame God here! How vigorous God is in his righteousness! Verses 5b and 6b sort of blow up the myth about God 'hating sin yet loving the sinner.' He does not hate the evil done but evildoers (5b); he doesn't detest merely bloodthirsty deeds but bloodthirsty men (6b). What holy, praise-worthy hatred! You do not pray to a bland blob. Yahweh has a certain *character*. And because David knows that character, knows what Yahweh loves and what he hates, he has real hope that he will come to his rescue.

How does this instruct us in our prayers? For one thing, it infects our prayers with praise. Look back over these verses (i.e., vv. 4–6). David is declaring Yahweh's character but, in doing that, he is at the same time praising Yahweh for the way he is. Sometimes I like to have our congregation begin a worship service with a confession of faith—like Article One of the *Belgic Confession*:

> We all believe with the heart
> and confess with the mouth
> that there is only one God,
> who is a simple and spiritual Being;
> he is eternal, incomprehensible, invisible, immutable,
> infinite, almighty, perfectly wise, just, good,
> and the overflowing fountain of all good.

Now you may think you are *only* confessing your faith with those words. But of course that is not the case. You *are* confessing your faith but you are also oozing into praise. You can't say those words and mean them without at the same time declaring both your belief and praising the God you believe in. That is the way in David's prayer: he rehearses Yahweh's character and in so doing he 'slips' into praise!

Then there is another bit of instruction: we must know what God is like before (or as) we pray. The character of God is the basis and springboard of our prayer. Some years ago while I was serving in academia I remember how a faculty associate was to meet with an administrator to argue his case about making certain changes in a departmental academic program. He was a bit worried that this administrator would be a 'tough nut to crack.' The faculty member, however, knew of an autobiographical memoir the administrator had written. So he got himself a copy of it and read it. He wanted to know everything he could about this administrative 'animal' so that he could press his case to the greatest possible advantage. And that is the case in prayer. Because Yahweh is the sort of God he is (vv. 4–6),

David can make particular kinds of petitions (for example, vv. 10–11). After all, why should you pray for some of the world's governments or leaders to be overthrown unless you know that your God hates oppression? Why pray for suffering Christians in hostile environments to be delivered unless you know a God who has said, 'I have surely seen the affliction of my people'? Know your God.

Make your request

Thirdly, the time comes to make your request (vv. 7–9). David prepares to make his request (1) on the basis of grace, 7a; and (2) in an attitude of reverence, 7b.

The pronoun ('But I...') in 7a is emphatic. David has just testified that Yahweh hates evildoers and detests bloodthirsty and deceitful men (vv. 5–6), so we might expect him to contrast his own superior resume and morality. But there is nothing of the kind. 'But I...,' he says, can enter your house only by 'your overflowing and faithful love' (lit., 'in the abundance of your unfailing love'). David does not come on the basis of his religiosity or his deserts but only by grace.

And he comes by fear. 'I will bow down toward your holy temple in the fear of you' (7b). What a combination we have here (as in all quality worship). In 7a we meet the welcome, friendship, and acceptance grace extends, and yet 7b reflects the majesty, kingship, and trembling that fear knows. Glad welcome and trembling reverence together. This reminds me of Andrew Bonar's story about the Grecian painter who had produced a remarkable painting of a boy carrying a basket of grapes on his head. It was so true to life, so realistic, that when the painting was displayed in the Forum, the birds pecked the grapes, thinking they were real. His friends praised the painter, but he was displeased. 'I should have done a great deal more. I should have painted the boy so true to life that the birds would not have dared to come near!' In short, he should have attracted them and repelled them all at one blow. So here; David is both lured by grace yet sobered by fear—just the right packaging for worship!

Now for the petition. It is the primary petition—and we get half-way into the psalm before we get to it. 'Yahweh, lead me in your righteousness because of those lurking for me; make your way straight before me' (v. 8). His danger— 'those lurking for me'—clearly drives his prayer; these enemies are bent on his destruction and will use deceit, even with its honey and sugar, to get it done (v. 9). So, he prays, 'lead me in your righteousness.'

But what does that mean? I take him to mean in this context 'the righteousness that you require of me,' the 'right way you want me to go.' In the next line he speaks of 'your way,' apparently a way of conduct he is to follow. Perhaps there's a subtle implication that, in this mess, walking in righteousness is even more critical than walking in safety. In any case, in view of the danger and deceit of his enemies, he needs to see the next step, the clear way in the muck of his circumstances, one that pleases Yahweh.

It's a simple and brief petition. One might say that its New Testament equivalent is Matthew 6:13 ('Do not lead us into temptation, but deliver us from the evil one'). Sometimes we may not be fully aware of all the details— not know all the particular dangers or various pitfalls, nor even the precautions required. Sometimes it looks like there are no roads in what's ahead of us. But we can pray verse 8.

Here's a lovely young wife. A servant of Jesus. Cancer. One day at the surgery ward and all of life has tumbled in on this young couple. In the sadness and tears and what-must-we-do-nows, how can I pray for them? How can they themselves pray? What prayer makes more sense in such anguish than: 'Yahweh, lead me in your righteousness… make your way straight before me'?

Declare your confidence

And then we might say that David's fourth direction would be: declare your confidence (vv. 10–12). He continues his prayer but gains confidence as he goes. Verses 10–11 contain his two-pronged petition: prayer *against* his and Yahweh's enemies in verse 10, and prayer *for* God's people, for their joy and protection, in verse 11. Would you pray as David does in verse 10? *Hold them guilty, O God! Let them fall because of their schemes; banish them for their many rebellious deeds.* Does it make you uneasy to pray like that? But you haven't any choice, for the petition of verse 11 cannot be answered unless that of verse 10 is answered; that is, God's people cannot enjoy security and safety (v. 11) unless—at some point—their enemies are taken out of the way (v. 10). What community can rest easy so long as a rampaging murderer-rapist has not been apprehended and punished? The New Testament carries the same testimony. Paul says to the battered Thessalonian saints that they will receive rest when—at Jesus' coming—God deals out affliction to those who are afflicting them (2 Thess. 1:6–7).

We may wish prayer could be all courtesy and finesse. If so, we've no business messing with the Psalms. Prayer must often have a hard edge about it, because it has to deal with evil. There's a *ruggedness* about true biblical piety. Why is the psalmist so ecstatic over Yahweh's coming to *judge the earth*? Because it means that at that time he will *put things right* ('he will judge the world with righteousness'); and only when that happens can the cosmic party begin (see Psalm 98:7-9).

In verse 12 David sets down the confident assurance on which his two-fold petition rests: 'For you will bless the righteous one, Yahweh; you will wrap him round with favor like a shield.' (This assurance is very similar to Psalm 1:6.) David does not know precisely when or how this will be done, but he knows who will see to it—the 'You' is emphatic; '*You* will bless the righteous one.' This security extends to the individual ('righteous' is singular here, not plural) and is complete (the word for shield, *sinna*, refers not to the hand-held but large, body-sized shield) and close (Yahweh 'wraps him round'). Derek Kidner refers to the other occurrence of this verb I have translated 'wrap round.' It appears near the end of 1 Samuel 23 when Saul almost has his meat hooks on David and his men. Saul on one side of a hill, David & Co. on the other side. David and his men are hurrying to get away from Saul, and Saul and his men 'were closing in' on David and his men to nail them (v. 26). He had surrounded David, was ready to wrap him up. Oddly enough, just at that moment a breathless messenger caught up with Saul with the news of a Philistine invasion—Saul had to let David go and go himself to defend his country. Saul had been closing in, but Yahweh was closer. The enemy cannot wrap us up when Yahweh has already wrapped us round with his favor.

In his autobiography German theologian Helmut Thielicke tells an incident from his earlier school days, when about ten years of age. He and his classmates had taken an intense dislike to another lad in their class. Hans exuded a kind of lackadaisical attitude toward studies and yet, when asked a question in class, he could spout off everything one might know about the matter. For this and other quirks Hans earned the ire of Thielicke and his friends. Hence they decided that the whole bunch of them needed to give Hans a thrashing. But on the morning set for the ambush, a strange thing happened. Hans' father was walking with his son that day to school. His father was one of the most highly respected men in town. The 'gang' noticed what happened when Hans and his father parted in front of the school. They saw how Hans' father stroked his son's hair and patted his cheek as they parted; then, several times as they both began to go their separate ways, father and son would turn and wave at each other. Thielicke said that he and his cohorts were very touched by this scene. It was as if they came to a collective, if unstated, conclusion: 'Whoever was loved by such a father stood under a protective taboo and could not be molested.' They were gripped by an unexpressed awe. And so Hans was spared. One might say he was wrapped round with favor as a shield!

So David ends his prayer with the confidence that nothing can finally hurt the righteous, for Yahweh's favor will always surround him. But what are we to do in the meantime, when we are living in an arrogant, deceitful, lying world, facing one pitfall after another? Keep praying the prayer the Lord has taught us to pray: *Yahweh, lead me in your righteousness because of those lurking for me; make your way straight before me.*

PSALM 6

For the music leader. With stringed instruments.
Upon the sheminith. A psalm of David.

1 Yahweh, don't rebuke me in your wrath!
    Don't chasten me in your hot anger!
2 Show grace to me, Yahweh, for I am withering;
    heal me, Yahweh, for my bones are terrified.
3 Yes, my soul is greatly terrified!
        But you, Yahweh—how long?

4 Turn back, Yahweh, rescue my life;
        save me because of your covenant love.
5 For in death no one remembers you;
        in Sheol who gives you praise?
6 I have become weary because of my groaning;
        all night long I make my bed swim,
        I dissolve my couch in my tears.
7 My eye has wasted away because of grief;
        it has grown old because of all my foes.

8 Turn away from me, all workers of wickedness!
        For Yahweh has heard the sound of my weeping!

9   Yahweh has heard my plea for grace!
       Yahweh will accept my prayer!

10   Let them be ashamed,
       Yes, let all my enemies be greatly terrified!
       Let them turn back,
          let them be ashamed all of a sudden!

Wet Prayer

Many of us are likely familiar with the 'ACTS' pattern for prayer: adoration-confession-thanksgiving-supplication. Not a bad guide, especially since it stresses that prayer is more than petition. But sometimes our neat formulas have to be smashed. It just won't do for us to stand on the sidelines here at the first verse of Psalm 6 and scold David with 'No, no, you can't do that; you forgot—that's supplication, and you have to save that for last.' Sometimes emergencies demand that we ditch recommended patterns. Sometimes we have to plunge right in with petition. As David does here. Let's track our way through this prayer, for it too teaches us to pray.

The agony he knows

Looking at the psalm from David's vantage point, we first run into the agony he knows (vv. 1–3). These verses constitute a sort of this-is-the-mess-I'm-in section. What is it that feeds his agony?

Probably the *problem of wrath* (v. 1). 'Don't rebuke me in your wrath! Don't chasten me in your hot anger!' Some think that David may only be saying that he doesn't want God to be angry that he is bringing this matter (his need for God's intervention) up again in prayer. However, I think it more probable that there may be some sin that God is chastening him for—or that David thinks that God is chastening him for. And David does not want Yahweh to deal with him severely but to moderate his anger. We'll come back to this.

He mentions the *problem of weakness* (v. 2): 'I am withering.' He is wiped out with it all. It's difficult to know sometimes whether these descriptions are literal and physical or mostly metaphorical and figurative. Verses 6–7 seem to point to some degree of physical exhaustion. Add to this the *problem of fear* (vv. 2b–3a). The verb in the text is not merely 'dismayed' or 'troubled' but rather 'terrified.' Both bones (2b) and soul (3a) are in this state—hence the whole person is terrified. What causes this terror? From the psalm it might be the disfavor of God (v. 1) or sickness (v. 2, 'withering...heal me') or the threats of enemies (vv. 8, 10)—or maybe all of the above.

And the *problem of time* contributes to his agony (v. 3b). This is one of our perennial problems with God's ways. We have our calendar. We have figured about how long we can hold out. And somehow Yahweh allows our urgent deadlines to pass. Why? David's 'How long?' means: How long will you allow this to go on? Why don't you intervene and give me relief? Why does he wait? Why does he hold off? When we say God will intervene sooner or later, why does it always seem to be later? Our troubles, it seems, are as much with God as with our circumstances.

But perhaps the most pressing of these matters is whether one is under the displeasure of God (v. 1). Is there any agony like the loss of the friendship of God? What can Yahweh's servant do when he is under Yahweh's wrath? Simply pray as in verse 2: 'Show grace to me, Yahweh...; heal me, Yahweh.' You go to the Bringer of wrath with a plea for grace. Where else can one go?

My father would tell of a particular occasion (as opposed to others!) when he spanked my oldest brother. Walt was a toddler and, for some apparently just reason, he came under the sway of the parental hand. My father was a pastor and had his study at the house. After the spanking he went back to his work. After a while, Walt came round the corner, into the study, crawled up on Pop's lap, put his arms around him and said: 'Papa, I love you.' I don't think we need to say that was 'sweet' or 'precious.' I think we need to think about how he was thinking. He seemed to be assuming, instinctively perhaps, that the hand that had struck him would nevertheless welcome him. Perhaps that's what drives David's plea in verse 2—he knows that the God who strikes him is often a 'striking and healing' God (Isa. 19:22).

The argument he brings

Secondly, we should notice the argument he brings (vv. 4–7). David both brings his petitions to God and presses his reasons upon God; in the middle of the emergency he argues his case; he tells Yahweh why he should and must deliver him.

The first argument has to do, David might say, with *the God I have*: 'save me because of your covenant love' (v. 4). This is an argument that rests on the character of God. 'Covenant love' here is *hesed*, the devoted love that pledges never to let go of us. David praises Yahweh for this in 2 Samuel 22:51; there he says that Yahweh is 'the tower of deliverance for his king, the One who keeps acting with devoted love [*hesed*] toward his anointed, to David and to his seed for all time.' True to his promise in 2 Samuel 7, Yahweh had brought nations to acknowledge David's supremacy (2 Sam. 22:44-9). This, of course, is simply a particular application of Yahweh's faithful character, for he is 'rich in *hesed* and fidelity' toward all his covenant people (Exodus 34:6). We might paraphrase David's petition as: 'Save me for you have pledged yourself to deal lovingly with me and I am holding you to your word.' It's an argument that rests on God's promise, or even beneath that, on his character.

Peter Collier tells of Theodore Roosevelt, Jr.; he had been in World War I and came back to fight in World War II as well. He was one of the few fighting generals the Americans had. He had been in North Africa and Italy, and then on the eve of D-Day he demanded that General Eisenhower allow him to go ashore with the first wave of attack at Utah Beach. He was fifty-seven years old, crippled with arthritis, having to use a cane to get around—and he wanted to hit Utah Beach. What was his argument? 'My men expect it of me. I'm the son of Theodore Roosevelt.' One could paraphrase: 'I have to—it's who I am; it's part of my character.'

That is David's argument here. He is resting in Yahweh's character, in the sort of God he had declared himself to be.

Sometimes this is your only stay in trouble—simply what God has said about himself and about what he will do. Which suggests how massively important the doctrine of God is for the Christian life.

David's second argument centers on *the praise I give* (v. 5): 'For in death no one remembers you, in Sheol who gives you praise?' The verb 'remembers' has to do with expressing praise in worship, as the next line of this verse makes clear. Sheol is the realm of the dead. This may make you antsy, but let me paraphrase what I think his argument is. It's as if he is saying: If I die, if I succumb, if my enemies get me, if you do not deliver me, there will be one less to praise you, for I won't be able to sing 'Praise ye the Lord, the Almighty, the King of creation' among your people; they don't sing 'O for a Thousand Tongues to Sing' in Sheol; dead folks don't get up and sing 'Let us love and sing and wonder, let us praise the Savior's name!' Now, let's not get on 'rabbit trails' here: this verse does not mean David had no hope beyond death, nor is it some form of bribery. Let us think about verse 5 in terms of what he is *assuming* here.

Assumptions are frequently revealing. Some time ago I was on the campus of a prominent evangelical seminary and while in one of the buildings decided to use the men's room. After I had washed my hands in the lavatory and reached for a piece of paper towel, I was startled by a sign attached to the towel dispenser: 'Please do not flush paper towels in the toilet.' Now I knew *why* the maintenance department did not want paper towels flushed down the toilet—they would clog up the drain; they were not intended to be disposed of that way. I began to think: Why was such a sign necessary? Why would anyone commit such an offense anyway since one would have to take the trouble to walk away from the waste paper container and go back to the toilets in order to do so? What was this sign saying about the propensities of the future pastors of evangelical churches in my country? Assumptions are revealing.

Now that is the case here. When David so much as says, If I end up in Sheol, I can't sing your praise, he is assuming that the whole purpose of his life is to praise Yahweh. That is a bit searching. Oh, I know in one way someone could say this is 'old hat,' because we have our cliché in our prayers about giving God all the glory, etc.; but this cuts deeper and is no cliché. This agonized prayer then tells you that your whole reason for existence is not to make a living, not to become the most outstanding servant of Christ possible, not to get a superb education, not to advance rapidly in your profession, nor to excel in the sport of your choice...but to praise God. David's prayer in verse 5 may expose you. How you answer the question, What's wrong with death?, will do it. The only correct answer is: Because then I wouldn't be able to stand at that padded pew at Woodland Presbyterian (or wherever else) and join my voice in singing, 'I greet thee who my sure redeemer art—my only trust and Savior of my heart'—because that is my whole reason for existence!

David's third argument underscores *the misery I know* (vv. 6-7). Here is the toll David's trouble has taken on him; he is emotionally and physically 'shot.' The groaning, the tears, the grief, the exhaustion—why does David rehearse all this to God? Does God need this information? What does this have to do with an argument in prayer?

Well (back to assumptions again), what is he assuming about God? He is making an assumption about the mercy of God. He is assuming that all of this really matters to

God and that Yahweh will be touched with pity over his condition. He assumes that our misery arouses God's mercy, touches God's heart. A prayer like this assumes that the Father is like Jesus—always going around being moved with compassion.

Perhaps these individual 'arguments' are of some help to us, but what general instruction should we derive from this matter of argument in prayer? That the use of argument is entirely proper in prayer, that it is beneficial, or even necessary! While I was teaching in seminary, I would sometimes have a student ask to take a scheduled exam at another time. Students (as a rule) knew that they couldn't simply tell me that they didn't feel up to an exam on a Wednesday. They knew a pitch like that would be turned down flat. They knew they had to make a 'case.' But if a student came in and told me that he had been reviewing for the exam but that two days ago his wife had gone into labor and was in the hospital with their second child, that while he had been with her, their two-year-old under a babysitter's care had fallen from a bunk bed and broken his arm, that his mother-in-law had been on her way to come help but the water pump had gone out on her car en route and she was delayed, and that he had not gotten more than forty-five minutes of sleep in the last two days, well then, one who had some modicum of mercy would allow him to re-schedule his exam.

I don't want to reduce prayer to an exercise in logic. But I would guess that too few believers give much thought to the use of arguments in prayer. No one can fail to see how highly emotional Psalm 6 is. And yet—with the place it gives argument in prayer—it is highly rational as well. Pushing ourselves to bring reasons for our requests may help us see how shoddy some of our petitions are—or it may encourage us if we seem to muster a cogent case. Argument in prayer shows that we are called to *thinking* worship.

The assurance he finds

Briefly and lastly, David's prayer shows us the assurance he finds (vv. 8-10). Verse 10 shows that the *actual* deliverance is still in the future; verse 10 is anticipatory—the decisive help has not yet arrived. And yet verses 8-9 show that he has *present* assurance of coming deliverance. On the basis of this assurance he defies his enemies (v. 8a). His assurance rests on the certainty that Yahweh has heard (vv. 8b-9):

> For Yahweh has heard the sound of my weeping!
> Yahweh has heard my plea for grace!
> Yahweh will accept my prayer!

Prayer doesn't change things, but prayer lays hold of God who changes things and who, in prayer, changes you. And sometimes in the midst of it all he gives you the assurance that your plea has been granted.

Notice especially David's terminology for prayer in 8b: 'the sound of my weeping.' *Yahweh has heard the sound of my weeping.* What a way to describe prayer. God can even make out what your tears long for. Shades of Romans 8:26 already! You probably ought to underline that; you can go through a lot with a text—and a God—like that!

Did you notice that strange heading to this psalm? All about the music leader and stringed instruments and perhaps the tune to be used? All of which implies the continued use of this psalm in public worship by the Lord's people. And why not? For there will be many of the Lord's flock post-David who also come with the sound of their weeping and will need the assurance that God will see their tears (cf. Isa. 38:5). And why shouldn't he? For he has given them a Savior, who, in the days of his flesh 'offered up both prayers and supplications with loud crying and tears' (Heb. 5:7)—and he was heard.

PSALM 7

*A shiggaion of David, which he sang to Yahweh
on account of the words of Cush, a Benjaminite.*

1 Yahweh my God, in you I have taken refuge
   —save me from all my pursuers and deliver me,
2 lest one tear me up like a lion,
   ripping (me) apart—with no one to deliver.
3 Yahweh my God, if I have done this,
   if there is unrighteousness in my hands,
4 if I have paid back my friend with evil
   (actually I have delivered the one
   who without cause is my adversary),
5 let the enemy pursue me,
   let him overtake and trample my life to the ground,
   and let him lay my glory in the dust. [Selah.]

6 Rise, Yahweh, in your anger,
   lift yourself up against the fury of my adversaries,
   and awake for me; you have appointed a judgment.
7 Let the assembly of peoples gather round you,
   and over it return on high.
8 Yahweh will judge the peoples;
   judge me, Yahweh, in line with my righteousness
   and in line with the integrity I have.

9 Oh, let the evil of the wicked ones come to an end,
  but give stability to the righteous,
  all the while testing hearts and feelings,
  O righteous God!
10 My shield is in God's hands,
  Savior of the upright in heart.
11 God vindicates the righteous,
  and God expresses anger every day.

12 If one does not repent, he will sharpen his sword;
  he has bent his bow, gotten it ready;
13 and for him he has prepared deadly weapons;
  he makes his arrows burning shafts.
14 Look! He is in birth pains with wickedness,
  and he conceives trouble,
  and gives birth to falsehood.
15 He has dug a pit, and scooped it out,
  —then fallen into the shaft he makes.
16 His trouble returns on his own head,
  and it's on his shoulders that his violence comes down.

17 I will give Yahweh thanks in line with his righteousness,
  and I will sing psalms to the name of Yahweh Most High.

[Note: the last half of verse 4 is very difficult; I have stolen freely
from Alec Motyer, *Treasures of the King*, 19]

Just Justice

7

James Bradley in *Flags of Our Fathers* remembers how very little his father would ever talk about what happened during the taking of Iwo Jima in World War II. Very close to the chest. And yet for an 'outsider' the very lack of information tweaks one's interest to know more. Take, for example, this allusion to 'Cush the Benjaminite' in the psalm heading. Who was this Cush? And what were the 'words'—apparently the slander—he spoke against David? But, like James Bradley's father, the psalm editors don't slake our curiosity. So we don't have all the background information we'd like, but we do have the prayer that came out of it all. And in this prayer David pleads for mere justice, or, as we might say, for just justice. Let's turn to his instruction.

Take care with your prayer

The first segment of the psalm tells us that we must be taking care with our prayer (vv. 1–5, and including the heading). David so much as says to Yahweh, Let me lay out before you my position [1a], my danger [1b–2], and my conscience [3–5]. 'In you I have taken refuge'—that is his position. His recent crisis has not driven him to this—he has been here all the time. The verb in the past indicates he has placed himself under Yahweh's shelter some time before this latest round of trouble. Yet for all that he stands in great peril—pursuers dog his tracks (1b) with all the finesse of a lion that rips prey and crunches bones (2); he will be helpless, and it will be messy and nasty.

And here's where he brings his conscience into the picture, as a way of maintaining his innocence (vv. 3–5). 'If I have done this' (3a), he begins. The 'this' is probably whatever it was that Cush the Benjaminite accused him of. So David says, If the slanders are really true, 'if there is unrighteousness in my hands' (3b), 'if I have paid back my friend with evil' (4a), then, he says, let the enemy pursue, overtake and trample me, and lay my glory in the dust (5). David is using a curse formula (If I have…then…) as a way of asserting his innocence of the charges, as a way of emphatically denying that any wrong action or hostility on his part has brought on this enmity. He is not claiming an across-the-board perfection; he is simply claiming to be clear of responsibility for this bit of trouble. But David is on terribly healthy ground in verses 3–5—he realizes that he stands under God's gaze and knows that God will know him truly.

I'm sure spying is becoming an ever-perfected art. But I was interested to find out how detailed it could be even in the 1970s. Jacques Derogy and Hesi Carmel (*The Untold History of Israel*) tell of the surveillance photos the CIA would take in the Middle East in the wake of the 1973 Yom Kippur War. They said that the shots are so sharp that a viewer can make out the time on a wristwatch worn by a soldier serving sentry duty in the Sinai. Nothing hidden. So God sees us in clear detail.

David knew he was under the searching scrutiny of Yahweh and submitted himself to it. It's as if David already knew of Hebrews 4:13: *Nothing in all creation is hidden from God's sight. Everything is uncovered and laid bare before the eyes of him to whom we must give account* (NIV). When we are conscious of that we take immense care with our prayer, since we realize with a holy and healthy trembling that every nook and cranny of our being is exposed to the searching analysis of heaven.

Find hope in God's anger

As David seeks for justice, we find him, secondly, finding hope in God's anger (vv. 6–11). 'Rise, Yahweh, in your anger' (6a). Now there is hope. If Yahweh in his anger pits himself against the 'fury of my adversaries,' well then, David says, I have hope of deliverance.

As David makes plain in verses 6b–8a, there is a doctrine that brings hope to tried and battered servants of God, and it is the doctrine of judgment. 'You have appointed a judgment', he prays in 6c, and in 8a he declares that 'Yahweh will judge the peoples.' He seems (in v. 7) to view the peoples being gathered as Yahweh himself sits as judge over them. The doctrine here nicely anticipates that of Paul's sermon in Athens: *He has fixed a day on which he will judge the world in righteousness by a man whom he has appointed; and of this he has given assurance to all by raising him from the dead* (Acts 17:31, ESV). There is a time coming when God will put things right.

If that is not the case, are we not led to despair? In late 1937 the Japanese entered China's capital, Nanking; they marched pregnant Chinese women to a killing field where the soldiers placed bets on the sex of the fetus about to drop out of a mother's womb when sliced open with a samurai sword. If they face no judgment how is their 'choice' any different from your choosing corn flakes over oatmeal for breakfast? Currently there are several warring factions within the Democratic Republic of Congo. Combatants of all groups, according to *WORLD* magazine, have had a long-standing practice of raping women and girls. Women are brutally gang raped, perhaps in front of their families, then frequently are shot or stabbed in their genital organs. If these thugs never have to face the bar of heaven, can their actions matter any more than attending the opera or changing the oil in one's car? David, however, has hope precisely because of Yahweh's anger, precisely because Yahweh has 'appointed a judgment.'

David seems to pray for a sample of the judgment to come in his current trouble: 'Yahweh will judge the peoples; judge me, Yahweh, in line with my righteousness' (v 8). When he prays 'judge me,' he means 'show me to be in the right.' He means: show me to be in the right in this Cush-the-Benjaminite-matter. 'God vindicates [lit., judges] the righteous' (v. 11), and David is asking Yahweh to do that for him in his present situation.

That is David's desire. But it's not all about David, as he makes clear in verse 9: 'Oh, let the evil of the wicked ones come to an end, but give stability to the righteous.' David's bout with unjust suffering, danger, and wrong stirs him up to ask God to suppress the evil of those who seek to crush Yahweh's people. His own trouble stimulated his prayers for the suffering people of God as a whole. And that should be the case with us, whether or not we ourselves are currently battling unjust oppression. Try to keep the trials of the 'persecuted church' before you on a regular basis. Think of the attacks of terrorist groups on the 3,000 Christians left in the Gaza strip; of the 'disappearance' of a North Korean girl and her family because she told her teacher it was 'by God's grace' she had gotten a good grade; of the way the Burmese army uses Karen Christian women and children as human minesweepers; and on it goes. But why? So you will throw up your arms and cry, 'Oh, let the evil of the wicked ones come to an end!' So it would stir us up to prayer for God's anger and justice to rush forth and work deliverance for his people.

'God expresses anger every day' (v. 11b). There are loads of people who will say that is not or cannot be true. But if you say that God is not like that, you take away any hope his wronged and suffering people have.

Watch judgment take place

Third, we find ourselves watching judgment take place in the lively scenario of verses 12–16. And first off David gives us a picture of Yahweh the warrior (vv. 12–13), a picture of God's judgment on the unrepentant. The 'he' refers to Yahweh. So if the enemy of the righteous does not repent and cease and desist, Yahweh will 'sharpen his sword' or he'll bend back his bow ready to take him out. That is the picture.

But then he takes us on to a process in verses 14–16, a process that Yahweh's judgment can take. The judgment may not be as direct as verses 12–13 seem to imply. In verse 14 he implies that wickedness may take some time to develop and show itself; it has a gestation period. And then judgment may come in a 'boomerang' and seemingly 'natural' manner; for example, the wicked man meticulously prepares his trap—digs and scoops out a pit, then makes a slight misstep and falls down the shaft he had planned for another (v. 15). 'His trouble returns on his own head' (v. 16a). But you must not think his downfall and ruin is simply the result of some natural law or bloodless principle. Behind the process of verses 15–16 stands the God of verses 12–13—his flaming arrows and razor-slicing sword bring the wicked to wreck.

Some years ago *Leadership* magazine carried an item originally from radio commentator Paul Harvey about the way an Eskimo kills a wolf, which is pertinent if grisly. First, the Eskimo coats his knife blade with animal blood and allows it to freeze. He adds several more layers of frozen blood until the blade is totally concealed. Next, he puts his knife in the ground with the blade up. When a wolf follows his nose and finds the bait, he licks it, tasting the fresh frozen blood. He begins to lick faster, with much more gusto, lapping at the blade until the sharp edge is bare. But now he is feverishly licking, harder and harder, his craving so intense that the wolf does not notice the sting of the bare blade on his own tongue—nor does he recognize the moment when his unquenchable thirst is being satisfied with his own warm blood. He craves more and more—until he's found dead in the snow next morning. God's judgment can work like that. The enemies of God's people give way to their passion to persecute, their lust to eliminate his servants. But then they begin to litter the field of history, felled by the Almighty's arrows, cut down by Shaddai's sword.

Remember praise is due

Lastly, David does not leave off his prayer without remembering praise is due (v. 17): 'I will give Yahweh thanks in line with his righteousness, and I will sing psalms to the name of Yahweh Most High.' This is not a bribe but a promise, a statement of obligation. When Yahweh vindicates David, he commits himself to give him the thanks and praise he should have. He agrees with Isaac Watts:

> O bless the Lord, my soul, nor let his mercies lie
> forgotten in unthankfulness, and without praises die.

My wife has a practice of taping up little scraps of paper to the inside of the window of the back door of our home. They are reminders of obligations or appointments or commitments she has. Something like: 'Tues., 3:30, take food to Mary.' Or maybe a dental appointment. Sometimes that window can get pretty cluttered, especially if she fails to remove fulfilled obligations. You might think she should use a calendar and write things down there. Well, she does; but she might not look at it! But if it's taped to the back door, it's hard to avoid. Verse 17 is David's back-door note; his personal 'post-it' note to not forget the praise he will owe.

It's all quite a cycle, isn't it? Trouble always leads to more psalms! Trouble drives us to God so that we can place it before him; then when he delivers from trouble we go back to him with praise. Whether in tears or in triumph, we never get away from worship, from having to deal with God.

PSALM 8

For the music leader.
To the Gittite melody [?]. A psalm of David.

1 Yahweh, our Lord,
   how majestic your name is in all the earth—
   where your splendor is recounted across the heavens!
2 Out of the mouth of children and infants
      you have established strength
      on account of your foes,
      to put an end to the enemy and the one seeking revenge.

3 When I look at your heavens,
      the works of your fingers,
      the moon and the stars which you have put in place,
4 what is man, that you pay attention to him?
   Or the son of man, that you show concern for him?

5 Yet you have made him a little less than God;
   and with glory and dignity you crown him.
6 You cause him to rule over the works of your hands;
   you have placed **everything** under his feet—
7 sheep and oxen—all of them,
   and even the wild animals,
8 the birds of the sky and the fish of the sea
     —whatever passes through the paths of the seas.

9 Yahweh, our Lord,
   how majestic your name is in all the earth!

Majestic Name

8

Have you noticed how the packaging of a product is meant to give you a specific impression? You may spot a bag of ginger snap cookies on the grocer's shelf—in some cases they are in a heavy brown paper bag, with plain lettering and no glitzy cellophane. The intent is to 'say': these cookies are an old-fashioned (the words may actually be on the package for the non-subtle purchaser), non-fancy, back-home, down-to-earth treat. The packaging means to give you that basic, back-to-grandma attitude about them. That is the way it is with Psalm 8, with its top and bottom 'wrapping' in verses 1a and 9. No, not to stir an appetite for cookies but to tempt you to delight over the splendor of God. By packaging the psalm within such wrapping David wants to excite you over the majesty of God and incite you to adore him for it. Then in the psalm David gives the reasons why you should be so taken with Yahweh's majesty. Of course, David speaks in the first person; but the heading of the psalm indicates its use in public worship—so David is assuming that what he says of Yahweh, you also will gladly say.

The irony of your strength

First, David says to Yahweh: you are to be adored because of the irony of your strength (vv. 1b–2). We usually pick up on irony when we see it; it's like a leaky pipe in a plumber's house, or when a worker for the national revenue service gets convicted for tax evasion. And David nails a bit of irony here: though Yahweh's splendor is splashed across the heavens, he has 'established strength' out of the mouth of children and infants, of all things. There is this contrast in the text between the foes, the enemy, the seeker of revenge and the children and infants, between these hairy-chested brutes who flex their muscles and show off their tattoos and these helpless babes. We needn't worry about whether David is thinking of a specific instance (or instances) or simply using a figure. The point is: what seems inconsequential has overwhelmed what is mighty.

What 'strength' is it that God establishes from the mouths of children and infants? It is likely the strength of *praise*—that's the way the Septuagint (the Greek translation of the OT) took it (see Matt. 21:15–16). So David is speaking of the lethal punch that praise packs; praise of God is highly powerful even if—or especially when—it comes from sources we would consider weak. There is a strange wallop in the praises of God's people that silences God's enemies. That seems to be the idea.

In this connection I think of how James Robertson describes the loss of T. J. Jackson (later, Gen. 'Stonewall' Jackson). His wife Ellie had given birth to a stillborn son, then she suffered an uncontrollable hemorrhage; in a brief time on a Sunday afternoon, Jackson's whole world caved in and he was utterly crushed. The next day he wrote his sister

Laura; he told her he thought he could submit to anything if God strengthened him for it; but he made no attempt to cover his sad despair. But then there in the middle of his note there is a most moving one-liner. He says: 'Oh! my Sister would that you could have Him for your God!' Can you imagine that? Can you think of anyone 'weaker' than Jackson, dashed and devastated by the Lord's 'taking away'? Here is a man beaten and crushed who nevertheless says, Oh! that you could have Him for your God. What defense does the suave, narrowed-eyed agnostic have for that? Sometimes the mightiest weapon in God's arsenal is not argument nor brilliance nor eloquence nor philosophy but praise. And the humblest believer can use it.

The mystery of your care

Secondly, David tells Yahweh: you are to be adored because of the mystery of your care (vv. 3-4). David considers all the data. He is not in a secular world: these are 'your heavens,' the 'works of your fingers,' heavenly bodies 'you have put in place.' David's is not a God-vacated world but a God-directed world. On a clear night David could likely see 2,000–3,000 stars. What if he'd had a good pair of binoculars? Up to 100,000. What if David knew (as Philip Yancey has put it in his book on *Prayer*) that if the Milky Way galaxy were the size of the entire continent of North America, our solar system would fit in a coffee cup, and that the Milky Way is one of perhaps 100 billion such galaxies in the universe? He probably would have been even more staggered than he was—but he had enough to stagger him, to be impressed with the massive vastness of his world over against his apparent insignificance. He considers this impressive data and yet holds to a marvelous truth: You 'pay attention to' man, you 'show concern for him.' He loses breath in saying it. When he exclaims, 'What is man?' he is speaking in baffled wonder and perplexed joy! Only the condescension of God can hold together astronomical vastness and individual concern. It gives David liturgical goose-bumps.

Of course, even pale reflections of such condescension amaze us. Patrick Kavanaugh tells of Mozart being accosted by a beggar in the streets of Vienna. The composer had no money to give, so brought the fellow to a coffee-house where Mozart quickly dashed off an entire Minuet and Trio, gave them to the fellow along with a letter, and sent him to his publishers. An astonished tramp soon possessed five guineas. Why didn't Mozart give him the buzz-off? Why should the fellow matter to him? Why should he care? Why invest time and effort?

'What is man…or the son of man?' Why should a mere speck of dust on the light years of God's calendar matter to him? David at least has no doubt that he *does* matter; he's just baffled to bits over *why*. When he says, 'What is man?', he is not asking a question but making an exclamation—he is really saying, 'What a God!' He is not posing a mental teaser; he is engaging in breathless praise.

The clarity of your revelation

Next, David tells God: you are majestic and adorable because of the clarity of your revelation (vv. 5–8). But why is it that David knows that God pays attention, that God cares, that his creature of dust, Man, matters to him? David says: Because the Bible tells me so. Note that verses 5–8 are simply a poetic summary of Genesis 1:26–31 (note especially verse 28). But some people never appreciate home until they try to run away from it—so you may not appreciate your Bible and you don't appreciate Bible answers unless you hear the other answers given—how they answer that question, 'What is man?', for not all ask that question with the hushed wonder and joy of David.

Consider the answer of paganism. I mean ancient, Mesopotamian paganism. Such a man-on-the-street pagan would say, 'When I look at the heavens, the moon and the stars, I fall down and worship them, for I believe they represent the powers of the universe; they are capricious and unpredictable—yet I am caught in their crunch, for they control my fate.' Check out the Babylonian 'creation myth', *Enuma Elish*; note there how *man is an accident*, how *man is a slave*; he is the garbage-man and janitor for the gods, doing the drudge work of providing the gods and goddesses with nourishment and satisfying their physical needs.

Or consider the answer of nihilism. What is man in the vastness of such a universe? He is nothing—only a piece of flickering warm rubbish at the dump, as important as a new-born maggot inside your garbage can on a hot summer day. *Man is junk.* James Sire (in *The Universe Next Door*) alludes to Samuel Beckett's play *Breath*. It's a 35-second play, no human actors. A pile of rubbish sits on stage, lit by a light that is dim at the first, gets some brighter but never fully so, then becomes dim again. No words; only a recorded cry at the first, an inhaled breath, an exhaled breath, and another recorded cry. Man is trash—trash that breathes momentarily, but trash nonetheless.

Or there is the answer of humanism. 'As in 1933,' says *Humanist Manifesto II* in 1973, 'humanists still believe that traditional theism, especially faith in the prayer-hearing God, assumed to love and care for persons, to hear and understand their prayers, and to be able to do something about them, is an unproved and outmoded faith.' 'We can discover,' they write, 'no divine purpose or providence for the human species.' We can't take space to dispute this, only to note it. They are simply saying that *man is alone*, and one gets the sense that they haven't the sense to see that that is sad.

But we have the answer of revelation in verses 5–8. When David asks 'What is man?' in verse 4 he is not cynical; he doesn't ask it with a curled lip; he asks it in wonder. Why does he know man counts? Where did he get that idea? That is, where did he get what he declares in verses 5–8? From reading his Bible, from Genesis 1—a word from *outside*. And that word says *man is royal*. God said: 'Let us make man in our image, after our likeness, and let them rule...' (Gen. 1:26). We don't take this position because we finally got it figured out, finally reasoned out what man's place is and so postulated that man is a higher form of life. No, God has stooped down and told us. Does this make a difference? Yes, it does. It makes a difference even in the assumptions one makes. Think of Jesus' word in Luke 12:24: 'Consider the ravens: they neither sow nor reap, they have neither storehouse nor barn, and yet God feeds them. Of how much more value are you than the birds!' That last statement—how does Jesus know that? Because Psalm 8 and Genesis 1 say so. Does it matter? Yes; it assumes that if ravens get road-kill the Father will surely see that you are sustained. After all, there's no comparison between ravens and royalty.

The certainty of your plan

Finally, David tells Yahweh: I want to praise you because of the certainty of your plan. Here I want to focus on verse 6 and draw in Hebrews 2:5–9 as well.

Well, it's all very nice (someone might say)—man ruling as Yahweh's vice-regent over his whole created order, but of course there's a big little word that makes the whole affair doubtful. And there it is in verse 6, the little word 'all' or 'everything' sitting like a sore, throbbing thumb in emphatic position in the text: 'you have placed *everything* under his feet.' But we don't see that. We don't see man ruling and controlling the whole created order; it seems more like cancer rules, or tragedies rule, or political tyrants rule. That's what the writer of Hebrews said. He quoted a bit of Psalm 8, including verse 6, and his response was: You know, we don't yet see that. *But we see Jesus!* His argument is: No, we don't yet see God's plan in final, living color, but we do see one man—Jesus! (Note our Lord's *human* name). Because of his suffering of death he has been crowned with glory and honor and reigns already over the whole created order (Heb. 2:5–9; cf. Eph. 1:22)! And he will bring many sons to glory to share in his reign. Man as such does yet enjoy the destiny mapped out in Psalm 8 but *One Man* does—and that gives us solid hope.

In *The Empty Cross of Jesus* Michael Green provides a helpful parallel for the situation in our text. He alludes to the speculation in European circles during the Middle Ages about whether there was a sea route to India, a way to the land of spices around the southern tip of Africa. No one could be sure, but many believed there was. Attempts at rounding that cape had failed—hence it was the Cape of Storms. But one sailor was determined to try once more. He succeeded in rounding the Cape and reaching the East. So ever since Vasco da Gama sailed back to Lisbon in triumph it has been impossible to doubt that a way to the East exists around what is now called the Cape of Good Hope.

That is the point of Hebrews 2. It says: Psalm 8 is not a pipe dream. We don't yet see it full-blown. But we see Jesus—one man is already reigning! And that is the assurance that redeemed man, his brothers and sisters, will one day rule as well. 'He has made them a kingdom, priests, to our God, and they shall reign on earth' (Rev. 5:10). How can you doubt your royal future when the Man Jesus has already begun enjoying it?

So, in light of these reasons, what should you do? The 'wrapping' of the psalm tells you. For a starter, why don't you fall down and say, 'Yahweh, our Lord, how majestic is your name in all the earth!'

PSALM 9

For the music leader. Upon Muth-labben. A psalm of David.

1   I will give thanks to Yahweh with all my heart;
    I will rehearse all your wonders.
2   I will be glad and elated in you;
    I will 'psalm' your name, O Most High.
3   When my enemies turn backward,
    they stumble and perish before you;
4   for you have maintained my just cause;
    you have sat on the throne dispensing righteous judgment.
5   You have rebuked nations;
    you have made the wicked perish;
    their name you have wiped out forever and ever.
6   The enemy has been finished off;
    they are ruins forever;
    and you have pulled down their cities,
    their very memory has perished.
7   But **Yahweh** sits enthroned forever;
    he has anchored his throne for justice.
8   And **he** will judge the world in righteousness;
    he will judge peoples uprightly.
9   And may Yahweh prove a high fortress
        to the one who is crushed,
    a high fortress for times of distress.

10 And may those who know your name trust in you,
    for you have not abandoned those who seek you, Yahweh.
11 Sing a psalm to Yahweh, enthroned in Zion;
    declare his deeds among the peoples;
12 for the One who tracks down bloodshed remembers them;
    he does not forget the cry of the afflicted.

13 Show grace to me, Yahweh;
    look at my affliction coming from those who hate me.
    You are the One who lifts me up from the gates of death,
14 in order that I might recount all your praises,
    that in the gates of Daughter Zion
        I might rejoice in your salvation.
15 Nations have sunk down into the pit they made;
    into the net they concealed their own feet have been caught.
16 Yahweh has made himself known
    —he has brought about justice:
    trapping the wicked in the work of his own hands.
    [Higgaion. Selah.]
17 The wicked will turn back to Sheol
    —all the nations that forget God,
18 for it's not forever that the needy will be forgotten,
    nor will the hope of the poor perish forever.

19 Rise, Yahweh! Don't let man domineer!
    Let the nations be judged before you.
20 Yahweh, make them a fearful spectacle
    —let nations know they are only men. [Selah.]

Throne Control

9

I had never done it before. But I thought it rather brilliant. I would cut down on my coffee-imbibing. So...I filled my thermos with ginger ale. But apparently the jostling as I carried my briefcase and thermos from the parking lot to my seminary office—not to mention the carbonation of my beverage of choice—was too much. By the time I was walking into our office area, ginger ale was seeping out the top of my thermos and drizzling to the carpet. I didn't realize what I was dealing with in ginger ale. And that's the way it is with Psalm 9. One can't be sure whether one is dealing with a psalm or half a psalm. Some think Psalm 9 goes with Psalm 10 to make up a whole psalm. There is no heading to Psalm 10, and there is a kind of broken acrostic pattern across the two 'psalms', that is, about every other verse seems to start with the next successive letter of the Hebrew alphabet. But that pattern is broken and is not complete. And besides, there is plenty to handle in Psalm 9, and so I am treating Psalm 9 as a complete psalm in itself.

The keynote of the psalm, in case your yellow highlighter is itchy, would be verses 7–8.

You might wonder, of course, about this strange-looking heading. What are we to make of that term 'Muth-labben'? We cannot be sure but it may be the name of the tune to which the psalm was to be sung. Congregations who have printed songbooks are accustomed to seeing the names of tunes noted with each hymn or psalm, e.g., Regent Square, Toulon, and so on. One impish composer (Ralph Vaughan Williams) wrote a tune and called it 'Sine Nomine,' Latin for 'without a name'! We use it with 'For All the Saints.' So here, 'Muth-labben' ('Death to [or, of] the son') may be an indication of the tune to be used in tabernacle or temple worship.

Pray in rememberance

Now, even if Psalm 9 is a half psalm, it is a prayer and instructs us to…pray in remembrance (vv. 1–12). Let's track David's train of thought and praise in these verses.

First off, he tells us 'what I have been through.' This is in verses 1–6 and focuses on experience. He begins with a burst of praise (vv. 1–2) and then rehearses God's deliverance (vv. 3–6), deliverance David received from nations who were fighting with him as Israel's king. This is what has taken place.

Next, David indicates 'where it's going.' This is in verses 7–8; this is a projection. David is saying something like this: My deliverances, my victories, are simply mini-demonstrations of where everything is headed, not naturally, but because *Yahweh* is the just king and will put things right at the last. 'And *he* will judge the world in righteousness; he will judge peoples uprightly' (v 8).

And so David can speak of 'what you can count on' in verses 9–12. This is assurance or testimony. Others then, he says, should be able to trust you (v. 10a) and to praise you (v. 11). And why? What do you *learn*, David might say, from my experience of his wonders and justice? We should always be asking that question.

It reminds me of the story about Harry Cohn's funeral. Cohn, the head of Columbia Pictures, died in 1958, and a huge crowd showed up at the funeral service. This was a bit mystifying since Cohn, for all his genius, had been dictatorial and nasty and had become universally loathed throughout Hollywood. When someone spoke to comedian Red Skelton about how surprised he was that such a large number of people turned out for Cohn's funeral, Skelton retorted: 'It just goes to show you, if you give the people what they want, they'll show up.'

That is the concern in the psalm—what is the it-goes-to-show-you point? Why should David have punched the replay button and told his story? The testimony, what we learn from it all, is in verse 10b ('for you have not abandoned those who seek you, Yahweh') and in verse 12 ('for the One who tracks down bloodshed remembers them; he does not forget the cry of the afflicted'). There is such a straight-up realism here: we are talking about those who have been crushed, those in distress (v. 9) and those whose blood has been spilled in violence (v. 12). And in face of that, verses 10b and 12 may seem like small potatoes to you, but these may be the very assurances that some of you need rubbed into your pain *this very moment*.

Pray in context

Secondly, David implies that we must pray in context (vv. 13–18). In this segment of the psalm you must be careful to pick out the basic pattern: a plea (vv. 13–14) followed by an assurance (vv. 15–18). Here is a fresh need, another emergency, in verses 13–14. And as he prays note how David goes back to what Yahweh has done for him before—note how verses 15–16 pick up verses 5–6; and note how verse 18 reinforces what he taught us in verses 10b and 12. Here's what seems to be happening: in verses 1–12 David remembers Yahweh's deliverance in a segment of his experience and gains the assurances of verses 10b and 12 from it; then, when facing more trouble (vv. 13–14), he takes those previous assurances (vv. 5–6 reasserted in 15–16 and vv. 10b and 12 in v. 18) to encourage his hope again. David's hope arises not just because of Yahweh's deliverance in a slice of his experience (vv. 3–6) but because that deliverance discloses the consistent way and character (vv. 10b, 12, 18) of a just and saving God. And since Yahweh is that kind of God, he prays in confidence. That is the context in which he prays. So we can make two observations.

The first observation is that *wonderful deliverances can be followed by fresh needs* (verse 13 coming, as it does, in the wake of the experience of verses 1–12). A believer's life does not consist of a jam or two, but normally of troubles all along the way. We should never be surprised that after a marvelous deliverance we are somehow in the middle of more slop.

The second observation is that of our main point, namely, that *in fresh troubles we must remember the context in which we pray.* Ignoring our context can prove disastrous.

Carl Erskine was a pitcher for the old Brooklyn Dodgers. He tells of a time when he was eleven years old. Carl's father had purchased a book on pitching baseball and was concentrating on learning (apparently for himself and Carl) to throw a decent curve ball. They were in the living room of their home, Mr. Erskine held the pitching book in his left hand and a baseball (naturally) in his right. He's reading and very engrossed in what he's reading/doing. The arm is to be carried back, the wrist cocked, at which position the arm is to come forward with a snap and a spin of the fingers. Carl's father goes through the whole process, staring at the book, and releases the baseball! The ball sails through the doorway to the dining room and into the big china cupboard with the glass front, breaking that glass and smashing dishes. Enter Mrs. Erskine. He had forgotten his context and it made for trouble.

So, in trouble and in prayer you must remember where you are. Note where David was: he was in a history with his God, who had delivered him in a slice of his experience (vv. 3–6), and far more: for that deliverance was typical of what Yahweh *will* do at the last (vv. 7–8) and also displayed his character, that is, the way he acts toward his afflicted ones (vv. 10b, 12, 18). Are you not also in a history with your God? Do you not also have such a context out of which you pray? That's why you need—if not a journal— at least a mental 'book of remembrance' (something like the equivalent of verses 1–12), a record of goodnesses and mercies you can readily recall or consult. Samuel had the right idea in 1 Samuel 7:12, when he set up that Ebenezer ('the stone of help') monument with the testimony, 'Up to this point Yahweh has helped us.' A believer has a two-track history to remember: redemptive history, the record of Yahweh's faithfulnesses to his people in the biblical story, and personal history, the multiple episodes of that same biblical faithfulness in one's own case. When you remember this context, you pray in hope. In face of new needs, you pray 'show grace to me, Yahweh, look at my affliction' (v. 13a) with the confidence that an ear is listening. Another trouble, or batch of them? What am I to do? Bring it to Yahweh, who heard you the last time and the time before that.

Pray in anticipation

Finally, David shows us that we must pray in anticipation, or, as we might put it, pray for the kingdom (vv. 19–20). Here David looks at the 'big picture'. The 'nations' are on David's mind in this psalm—he mentions them five times (vv. 5, 15, 17, and then here, in 19 and 20). He also speaks of the 'world' and the 'peoples' in verse 8. The conflicts David rehearses through the psalm may have mostly come from surrounding nations attacking him and his having to defend against them. But here at the close of the psalm David prays for Yahweh to write 'Finis!' on the raging of the nations; he asks Yahweh to put down the arrogance and the swaggering of the nations. His prayer is simply, 'Thy kingdom come!'

This still needs to be our plea. The hands of nations and governments—in the past and today—are stained up to their shoulders in the blood of Christ's people. In Soviet days we heard of Christians being treated with drugs in psychiatric hospitals, made to veer out of their minds, and then declared 'insane.' In India, Orissa state, Hindu extremists attacked and burned Christians' homes, churches, and belongings. Over 100 people were killed in this butchery and 70,000 left homeless or in refugee camps. Only twenty-four assailants have been convicted—nearly four times that many have been acquitted.

Or in Myanmar (Burma) there are twenty Christian families who walk to church once a week (it takes a whole day each way, with children along); they have been attacked six times by the Burmese army. And so we pray verses 19–20; we ask for the kingdom of God to come; we ask for the judgment of God to take place, for the strutting nations and rulers of the earth to know that they are not gods after all.

In the earlier part of the Battle of Gettysburg (July 1863) in the American War between the States, things were one confusing mess behind the Federal lines. Ambulances clattering along, dazed stragglers wandering around, the deafening sound of big guns, the crackle of small arms, the yelling and screaming of men. There was, Bruce Catton tells us, a column of General Slocum's troops marching toward the firing line, a line they still could not see. The high screech of the Rebel yell rather unnerved them. They were veterans, but there was something about the ungodly racket they heard that put them on the edge of panic. They were passing a little cabin by the roadside and in front of it was a bent old woman. She sensed the unease of the troops and as rank on rank passed her, she kept soothingly repeating, 'Never mind, boys—they're nothing but men.' One soldier said that these commonplace words uttered in that context seemed almost sublime, and the lads shook off their panic and were brave soldiers once again.

And that is what we must always remember—long before the nations finally learn it. The nations are 'only men.' The power in Beijing or London or Washington or Moscow or Tehran or Caracas or Havana is nothing but flesh. Praying for the kingdom will force us to remember that.

You may have only half a psalm in Psalm 9 (who knows?), but you have plenty here to assist you in directing your pleas to your God, to pray in remembrance, pray in context, and pray in anticipation. You also pray in hope, for, after all, the throne (v. 7) is occupied.

PSALM 10

1 Why, Yahweh, do you stand a long way off?
  Why do you hide in times of distress?
2 In (his) arrogance the wicked is in hot pursuit
      of the lowly
    —let them be caught in the schemes they have concocted!

3 For the wicked boasts over his soul's desire,
  and the greedy curses—he holds Yahweh in contempt.
4 The wicked in his conceit (thinks),
      'He will not track it down.'
    'There is no God' is the sum of his thinking.
5 His ways prevail at all times,
  your judgments are high—out of his sight;
  as for all his adversaries, he blows them off.
6 He says in his heart, 'I will not be shaken';
  'From age to age I am the man who is never in trouble.'
7 His mouth is full of cursing—as well as deceit
      and oppression;
  under his tongue—trouble and wickedness.
8 He sits in ambush in villages;
  in hidden spots he kills the innocent;
  his eyes stalk the unprotected.

9 He waits in ambush in a hidden spot,
       like a lion in its lair;
    he waits in ambush to grab the lowly
    —he grabs the lowly as he drags him off in his net.
10 He crouches, he hunkers down,
    and the unprotected falls into his claws.
11 He says in his heart,
    'God has forgotten,
    he has hidden his face,
    he never, ever sees!'

12 Rise, Yahweh!
    O God, lift up your hand!
    Do not forget the suffering!
13 Why should the wicked man hold God in contempt?
    He says in his heart that you will not track it down.
14 You have seen! Yes, you have!
    You take note of trouble and aggravation,
       to place (such matters) in your power.
    The unprotected abandons himself **to you**;
    you have been the orphan's helper.
15 Break the arm of the wicked and evil man;
    track down his wickedness until you find no more of it.
16 Yahweh is king forever and ever!
    Nations shall perish from his land.
17 You have heard the desire of the suffering, Yahweh;
    you will settle their hearts;
    you will bend down your ear;
18 to put things right for the orphan and
       the one who is crushed,
    that man who is of the earth might not strike terror
       any more.

HIDDEN HEARER

Living here in the 'pine belt' of southern Mississippi I periodically have to clean pine needles off the roof of our house. I've found that the easiest way to do this is to take our gasoline blower up on the roof and blow the needles off the roof, then get down and rake them up in the yard. Why do I do such a chore? Well, usually because it's the next thing on my list. It may come after putting out the trash and changing the furnace filters. It's simply the next item to do. Psalm 10 is something like that. We're trying to give a brief exposure to the first twelve psalms—and Psalm 10 is next. One usually doesn't study Psalm 10 because it is one's favorite psalm. Have you ever heard anyone say that Psalm 10 is his/her favorite psalm? But this, you see, is the value of working through chunks of biblical material. You are forced to wade through what you might otherwise avoid; so you deal with Psalm 10 because it is next, not necessarily because it tweaks your attention or tempts you with its sometimes torturous Hebrew. I don't need to ease you into this psalm by talking about some 'need' you have. Verse 1 lays it out. You've been there. Let's jump in. There are three segments to the psalm and each can be summed up in one word.

Lament

The first segment is lament (vv. 1–2). Very abrupt. Verse 1 smacks you in the literary nose right off the bat: 'Why, Yahweh, do you stand a long way off? Why do you hide yourself in times of distress?' If you arrive at Psalm 10 straight from the companion psalm, Psalm 9, this is a bit of a shock. For, on the whole, Psalm 9 is rather positive. But here is the polar opposite experience, which tells us that there are 'seasons' in a believer's life—and sometimes the seasons suddenly change.

I attended college in a smallish town called Sterling, Kansas. Anyone who lives in Kansas knows that the air is always moving—either from the south or from the north. A south wind normally means warmer temperatures, a north wind colder ones. I recall one day, probably in the late fall, with the wind from the south and the temperature was 78 (sorry, I only understand Fahrenheit); but the wind changed and came from the north, and next day it was 13. A sudden switch in circumstances—a believer's life can sometimes be that way.

Our psalmist is nothing but candid about this. It's an emergency situation with the wicked in 'hot pursuit' (2a) and his double 'Why?' doesn't mince any words. His complaint is both accusing and encouraging. His 'whys' imply that God is acting in a way that's out of character for him (or should be), and yet the pray-er has the freedom to express his frustration with God's ways.

I especially want you to see, however, that this lament is *faithful*. But let me digress a moment to explain a detail of verse 2. You may note that the NIV takes 2b as a description of the lowly/weak being caught in the wicked man's schemes. My translation takes it as a petition for the wicked to be caught in his own schemes. One can justify either translation. I prefer the latter (with NKJV and NASB). So he erupts with this one-liner prayer: 'Let them be caught in the schemes they have concocted!' (v. 2b). And he prays that because the wicked is ready to smash God's lowly one (v. 2a). And that may not be so surprising or shocking if God didn't seem so indifferent and nonchalant about it (v. 1). You can even see a shred of faith in the double 'Why?' of verse 1, for behind that 'why' is the implicit recognition that Yahweh seems to be acting out of character. This is not what one expects from Yahweh, it's 'abnormal'—which simply says that the psalmist knows and has experienced what is normal for Yahweh. Hence this 'why' tells us that there has been a previous time of enjoying the consistency of Yahweh, a time in which faith was supported instead of perplexed. So even the 'why' presupposes faith; if there were no faith, why ask 'Why?'

But the petition in the last of verse 2 also shows this is a faithful lament. He not only asks why, but he also keeps pleading his own petition ('let them be caught...'). Faith is perplexed (v. 1) and yet goes on pleading (v. 2). The psalmist does not use God's baffling him as an excuse for disengaging with God but as an incentive to press on with him.

The problem then is with the 'hidden-ness' of God, with his apparent lack of intervention when man free-wheels in wickedness and in crushing the Lord's own. But here once more we see why this is a faithful complaint. Note carefully how verse 1 reads (I know this is below elementary but bear with me): 'why do you stand a long way off' and 'why do you hide yourself.' You notice the second-person address? What does this tell us? This is not a philosophical discussion in a university dormitory—it is prayer. He does not begin with, 'If God is both almighty and good, then why...', but with 'Why do *you*...' (emphasis mine). This is not merely some intellectual quandary but a devotional dilemma (which means it is a matter of faith). He does not understand Yahweh, but he is still dealing with Yahweh— and that is being faithful.

Description

The second segment of the psalm is description in verses 3–11. And it is a long description, speaking of the 'wicked' (the word is singular) and covering (1) his immunity, verses 3–6 (at least this is *his* view, cf. 'I will not be shaken,' 6a); (2) his ingenuity, verses 7–10 (e.g., 'he waits in ambush in a hidden spot,' 9a); and (3) his philosophy, verse 11 ('God has forgotten...'). Notice, by the way, that the 'wicked' in Psalm 10 (whether it refers to a particular wicked man or a 'representative' wicked man) must refer to another Israelite man—he is not from the 'nations' as in Psalm 9, for here he ambushes folks in the villages (v. 8).

But why this description of the wicked? Why take this time and space for him? Why give him all this press? We might make various guesses. We might say, for one thing, that these verses show how one's thinking (or 'heart'; vv. 4, 6, 11) determines and directs one's actions (vv. 8–10). But I think perhaps Derek Kidner has hit on the best reason here. He says that here in the psalm God is far off (vv. 1–2), the tyrant is doing nicely (vv. 3–11), and it 'is a function of the Psalms to touch the nerve of this problem and keep its pain alive, against the comfort of our familiarity...with a corrupt world' (Psalms 1–72, 71). The writer spills this ink on the wicked to keep the pain alive, to make us uncomfortable, to remind us that as Yahweh's servant you stand over against a whole world.

We can, of course, forget that. Barbara Tuchman tells of the arrival of Prince William Henry (later King William IV) in New York, on September 24, 1781. The place came to life as the British brass entertained the king's son. There were parties, receptions, parades, tours of the city and reviews of various regiments, dinners and concerts. The only problem was that General Cornwallis was besieged by the Americans and French at Yorktown and was waiting in vain for relief. So in New York they partied and in Yorktown (in less than a month) 8,000 surrendered. They forgot they were *at war*.

The believer's life is a war, a life-long conflict, and pieces like Psalm 10 are meant to aggravate you, to anger you, to sadden you—to keep you from forgetting that your life is always at odds with the wicked. Are not then these descriptions—of the wicked having such success trampling the helpless—meant to disturb and upset us and therefore drive us to prayer?

Intercession

All of which brings us, naturally enough, to intercession (vv. 12–18). The psalmist erupts in prayer: 'Rise, Yahweh! O God, lift up your hand! Do not forget the suffering!' (v. 12). He pleads the case for Yahweh's helpless people, and, as he does so, you sense that he is gathering hope. He finds hope, for example, in *the Lord's sight* (vv. 13–14). Verse 14 ('You have seen! Yes, you have! You take note of trouble and aggravation...') functions as the retort to the cocky security the wicked expresses in verses 4, 11, and 13.

In 1999 near Harrisburg, Pennsylvania, Kenneth Cains stumbled into the street and was hit by a dark Jeep Cherokee, which sped off. A coroner's report revealed that Cains was drunk. The driver of that vehicle was Thomas Druce, an up-and-coming Republican lawmaker in the Pennsylvania legislature. He told friends he had been in a minor accident; he told the insurance company he had hit a barrel on the Pennsylvania turnpike (that road is always 'under construction' somewhere). But the police received an anonymous tip in a Christmas card, of all things, and months later Druce was questioned, taken in, and sentenced to two to four years in prison. It had seemed like Druce was 'home free,' as we say, but someone had seen. 'Can anyone hide somewhere secret without my seeing him?' (Jer. 23:24, NJB).

Encouragement also comes from *the Lord's reign* (vv. 15–16). If verse 16a ('Yahweh is king forever and ever!') is true, then both nations (v. 16b) and the wicked (v. 15) will be put down under Yahweh's justice. Yahweh both is king and will prove to be king—this is non-negotiable truth and is true no matter what the wicked do right now.

Maxie Dunnam once wrote of the time when novelist Lloyd C. Douglas was a university student. He lived upstairs in a boarding house. Downstairs on the first floor lived an elderly, now infirm, retired music teacher. According to Douglas, they had a morning ritual. Douglas would come down the stairs, open the old man's door, and ask, 'Well, what's the good news?' The elderly gent would pick up his tuning fork, tap it on the side of his wheelchair, and say: 'That's middle C! It was middle C yesterday; it will be middle C tomorrow; it will be middle C a thousand years from now. The tenor upstairs sings flat, the piano across the hall is out of tune, but, my friend, that is middle C!' And God's ravaged but believing saints know that Yahweh's kingship is a far more stubborn datum than middle C.

And then encouragement comes through *the Lord's strength* (vv. 17–18). Our petitioner is confident that Yahweh has heard 'the desire of the suffering' and from that he infers a double assurance: 'you will settle their hearts' and 'you will bend down your ear.' The fact that 'Yahweh has heard' will lead to his '[putting] things right for the orphan and the one who is crushed,' as verse 18 indicates. However, it seems like the double assurance of verse 17 may be looked upon as what Yahweh does even before he finally puts everything to rights as in verse 18. Derek Kidner put it this way: 'Meanwhile, however distant may be the day of justice, one promise is not delayed: *thou wilt strengthen their heart*' (which is the RSV equivalent of our 'you will settle their hearts'). How much we need such assurance—not only of the final solution (v. 18) but of the stamina to stay on our feet until that time comes (v. 17b). Though we are not apostles, many of us understand when Paul makes the same point in 2 Timothy 4:16–17 (NIV): 'At my first defense, no one came to my support, but everyone deserted me...but the Lord stood at my side and gave me strength.'

Strange, is it not, that as one prays for God's people in their need one naturally has to focus on Yahweh himself, and so as you pray you are encouraged because you see his perception (vv. 13–14), position (vv. 15–16), and power (vv. 17–18)?

Before his death, Jesus told his disciples, 'I will not leave you orphans—I will come to you' (John 14:18). And he did—in his resurrection appearances they saw him again. Yet there may be a sense in which Jesus still says that to his people— when he comes again and brings the fullness of his kingdom and 'puts things right for the orphan and the one who is crushed.' Across this earth wicked man revels in trying to strike terror into Jesus' people—denying basic rights, torturing and imprisoning them, pillaging and ravaging at will, bleeding them dry, as it were, with unceasing cruelty. Yet these despised people have a firm assurance from their watching King: 'I will not leave you orphans.'

PSALM 11

For the music leader. Of David.

1 In Yahweh I have taken refuge.
  How can you say to me,
  'Flee, O bird, to your mountain,
2 for look, the wicked are bending the bow,
  they have placed their arrow on the string
  to shoot in the dark at the upright in heart
3 —when the foundations are thrown down
  what can the righteous do?'

4 Yahweh is in his holy temple;
  Yahweh—his throne is in the heavens!
  His eyes gaze on,
  his eyelids test the sons of men.
5 Yahweh tests the righteous,
  but the wicked and the one who loves violence
      his soul hates.
6 He will rain down snares upon the wicked;
  fire and sulfur and a scorching wind will be
  the portion of their cup;
7 for Yahweh is righteous,
  he loves righteous deeds;

  the upright will gaze on his face.

CRUMBLING FOUNDATIONS *11*

Years ago one of John Lawing's 'What if' cartoons in *Christianity Today* depicted Martin Luther at the Diet of Worms, making his answer: 'Here I stand, at present, I think, but then again, I could be wrong.' A deliberate parody. Still it may contain a grain of truth—that matters are seldom as stable and firm as we may think. At least that's the case in Psalm 11 where David's friends (apparently) are speaking of 'the foundations' being 'thrown down' (v 3). What does that mean? From the contents of the psalm itself it at least means a time when all the normal protections and securities for God's people disappear. It may indicate a time when the social fabric of life is disintegrating and all the glue seems to be going out of whatever normal civil order seems to be. *Today's English Version* puts it this way: 'There is nothing a good man can do *when everything falls apart.*' What becomes of our faith-position in such times? Or can we have one? We don't know what precise situation David was facing here, nor do we need to know, in order to face the main question of Psalm 11: What can the righteous do, what can faith do, when (as some say) everything is falling apart? Let's track the faith through the psalm.

The advice faith hears

First, we need to notice the advice faith hears (vv. 1–3). Of course, this 'advice' is not what we first hear. Rather we hear David's own position: '*In Yahweh* I have taken refuge.' As the marking indicates, 'in Yahweh' is emphatic in the Hebrew text. Here is David's anchor. He at any rate is not at sea. The 'foundations' may be torn down but this foundation remains.

Then we have to answer a question about the text. After his opening 'position-statement' David goes on with 'How can you say to me...,' and goes on to quote someone. Check your translation to see how much it includes in the quote. There are some translations and/or expositors who limit the quotation to verse 1c (Calvin, NBV, NKJV); others extend it through verse 2 (NEB/REB); while a good number see the quote running through verse 3 (JB, NIV, NASB, TEV, ESV). I think the last is the best option here. You notice that the speaker refers to the 'wicked' (pl.) in the third person, which tells us that whoever is speaking distinguishes himself/themselves from the wicked. These then are most likely friends of David whom he quotes here. Of course, he could be summarizing the rising thoughts of his own heart, but I think it more likely these are friends and associates speaking, as if to say, 'The wicked are going to nail you, in fact, everything is falling apart, and your best bet is to hightail it to some remote hide-out and hunker down there.'

What you hear in vv. 1c–3 is the advice of fear; it is sane, but it is in conflict with v. 1a—and David clearly senses that ('How can you say to me...?').

Why does this matter? What is the importance of this? Well, it is important because of the *source* of this advice which in turn makes it so subtle. This advice is coming from someone who cares about you (as these cared for David's security), not from some obvious opponent. Not long ago there was an advertisement in a Christian magazine for a particular Christian college prep school. Its ad shows a young man at university, sitting at a table in the library with an attentive, attractive co-ed. The caption to the ad reads: 'Where is your son getting his answers? Maybe from a sweet girl like Julie. She is smart, pretty, and believes she is a reincarnated Babylonian princess.' The concern of the ad implies the subtlety of the situation; the danger doesn't come from a fire-breathing, faith-destroying ogre but from an 'easy-looker' to whom you are forming an emotional attachment. That is somewhat the situation in the psalm. The danger comes from someone beside you. For David, of course, these were not folks who believed they were reincarnated Babylonians! But they were folks who cared about him, who wanted to be by his side, wanted to support him. Verses 1c–3 is not the advice of the wicked or a hypocrite or of an agnostic seeking to destroy you but of a Christian friend seeking to help. Yet for all that, it is basically opposed to faith. That's the problem with the counsel of verses 1c–3—it is pious, sincere, caring, concerned, and therefore, plausible. How this calls for the believer's discernment!

Haven't you faced this dilemma if you're a Christian? You can't tell whether a projected path is prudence or unbelief.

How do you tell the difference between a Matthew 10:23 situation ['When you are persecuted in one place, flee to another...'] and a Psalm 11 one? When should you run, when should you stand? When should you flee, when should you fight? When should you seek cover—or should you risk danger? The most religious, well-intentioned counsel may lead to living via unbelief. How can we tell the sane and the unfaithful apart? How we need that ability to 'discern what is best' (Paul's prayer in Phil. 1:9–10).

I recall a seminary student once coming in to see me looking for help with a queasy church situation. He was working as a youth worker in a congregation where there was conflict and dispute. He seemed minded to leave his post. What did I think? Since my own philosophy of ministry is that no problem in the church is so severe that it can't be run away from, I tended to agree with him. Fortunately, he spoke with another faculty member, who advised him to stick it out. As it turned out, that was the right advice. I wasn't trying to do that student harm or to lead him astray; still, I didn't chart the right way for him. H. L. Ellison has said it well: *The love of your friends will often create your most subtle temptations.*

Now we need to note one more problem with this advice before we move on. Don't miss the *assumption* behind this advice. It assumes that safety is all-important. Self-preservation is important, but when I assume it is all-important I have made it an idol. Am I doing that when I may think that I must retain the security of that job or of that status? We have probably crossed the idolatry-line when we think we should take no risks. It is possible to make such an idol of security that you prize it more than

God. The first line of this psalm says that in Yahweh I am as safe as I ought to be.

The answer faith gives

In sharp contrast to this fearful counsel we hear the answer faith gives (vv. 4–7b). You can catch the contrast if you place verse 2a over against the keynote of verse 4: 'For look, the wicked are bending the bow' versus 'Yahweh...Yahweh....'

So we see this picture in verse 4:

Yahweh is in his holy temple;
Yahweh—his throne is in the heavens!
His eyes gaze on,
his eyelids test the sons of men.

And we may be tempted to say: 'How can that help? That's just what I was afraid of—he's light years away!' But note the imagery, especially about the throne, eyes, and eyelids. David replies that his picture does not imply Yahweh is *removed* but that he *rules* (throne); that throne is not the place of *inactivity* but of *supremacy*; it does not suggest *distance* but *dominion*. Yahweh's exaltedness or 'transcendence' doesn't indicate distance or indifference but *activity* (gaze, test), which leads to judgment.

If Yahweh then is at the center of your vision (v 4), what do you see? In a word, his character. You see how just he is—the last half of verse 4 implies his judgments are just because they are based on careful testing and scrutiny (gaze, test). In the following verses you see how passionately just Yahweh is. Verse 5 may vary in the English translations, in the way the text is divided. My rendering follows the lead of the accents in the traditional Hebrew text—hence the last half of the verse reads: 'but the wicked and the one who loves violence his soul hates.' You may need to revise your theological clichés, about God hating the sin but loving the sinner! He hates, so he will rain down a raging retribution (verse 6). Yet Yahweh 'loves' (v. 7)—'he loves righteous deeds.' He hates, he loves. As in Psalm 5, you see how 'alive' he is?

All of this tells us that God is not a mere three-letter word. The God of the Bible is not a formless blob of celestial protoplasm, not some sort of cosmic jello with a sickly smile. He has a nature, a character, positive and negative. He is not the grand relativist but the living extremist. Let the flaming passion of these words slither down the throat of your soul and see how different this virile biblical God is from the sentimental deity men imagine. There is nothing bland about Yahweh.

Yahweh's righteous character (7a) explains his just judgment (vv. 5–6). And, once more (since we've seen it in other psalms), this justice is our only solid comfort and hope. If the righteous (as David & Co. in this psalm) are to be delivered the wicked must be judged (and that will only happen if God is actively just). That's why God's judgment is such *good* news for God's people; only when God comes and puts everything right can there be a universe party (Ps. 96:10–13) and only then can the Lord's people have rest (2 Thess. 1:6–9).

For the last few months the right front tire on my pick-up truck has been losing a bit of air every so often. Maybe 3–5 pounds of air pressure every week or two. So about every week I have to check the air pressure in that tire and often inflate it a bit. I was in Singapore recently for a couple of weeks. I left my pick-up at the airport when I left. When I came back, the first thing I did in the airport parking garage was to put my air gauge on that tire. I even had my portable inflator in the truck in case I needed it. I hate doing that—pampering along a slow-leak tire. I can hardly wait till it goes flat or gets ruined or wears out so that I can replace it with a new one that doesn't need nursing care. That is the Bible's position. The 'tweaking' has to stop sometime; God's people will only have ultimate comfort if they know he is going to 'take out' their oppressors. Until the enemy is destroyed they have no genuine security. People may bemoan the doctrine, but unless there is decisive judgment there is no solid salvation.

Now, before we leave faith's 'answer,' we must go back to its keynote in verse 4, for it is here that David reveals the secret of steadfastness in his chaotic world. This will seem too simple. (I mentioned it at the first of this point). Everything depends on your vision; you can either look at the wicked (v. 2a) or place your eyes on Yahweh (v. 4). Despair is managed by keeping Yahweh himself at the centre of your vision: 'Yahweh is in his holy temple; Yahweh—his throne is in the heavens' (v. 4a). That is all that anchors you when the foundations turn to slime.

Not long ago I received a report from a friend who does mission work in one of our Midwestern cities. He had taken a Christian man, an émigré from Egypt, to an appointment with a doctor. This man had been in the hospital six times in three months for liver failure and was a candidate for a liver transplant. In answer to the doctor's questions at this particular appointment, the Egyptian brother replied, 'Jesus here [pointing to his heart]; everything OK.' He was simply saying that there is something basic that controls the outlook on anything else in life. Same principle in Psalm 11. If verse 4 grabs hold of you, you can say, simplistically yet truly, 'Yahweh reigns; everything OK.' All of which explains Revelation 4, doesn't it? Why does John pummel us with 12 references to a throne (in the singular) except that he wants to steel his readers with the steadfastness they'll need in the chaos to come?

The assurance faith holds

We must not leave this psalm without noting the assurance faith holds (v. 7c): 'the upright will gaze on his face.' Derek Kidner has said it well: 'If the first line of the psalm showed where the believer's safety lies, the last line shows where his heart should be. God as "refuge" may be sought from motives that are too self-regarding; but to *behold his face* [RSV] is a goal in which only love has any interest.' There are many who are interested in safety, but only saints care about fellowship. The genuine disciple doesn't want only protection from God but communion with God. And such full and final communion is David's assurance here.

But, of course, even post-cross and post-empty tomb believers do not enjoy this hope yet. Peter catches our position in his striking description of Christians: 'though you have not seen him, you love him' (1 Peter 1:8). That is an astonishing thing. I think, for example, of the congregation to which I usually preach. I could very properly say to them: 'You—like myself—have never seen Jesus; and yet, in spite of that fact, there are many of you who would gladly confess that you love him. You have not seen Jesus yet you love Jesus.' Christians are such conundrums.

Years back there was a story in the *Presbyterian Journal* about a certain William Dyke, a Britisher, who was blinded in the earlier years of his life by an accident. Though handicapped, he threw himself into things, studied hard, and made an enviable academic record. He also courted a beautiful girl, who, in spite of his disability, consented to unite her life with his. Sometime before the wedding date, Dyke's case came to the attention of a skillful surgeon who suggested that there might be something that could be done for Dyke to recover his sight. He put himself into the hands of the surgeon, the surgery was performed, and on the very day of the wedding the bandages were removed. The surgery had been successful—he could see once more! Hence it happened that he saw his bride for the first time when they met at the front of the church sanctuary—what a moment of joy! And yet, in one sense, it was simply the proper fulfillment of all that had gone before. He had already held her hand, heard her voice, prized her love—now he saw her face. But he loved her before he ever saw her.

The same is true of the Christian—but the sight is coming (Rev. 22:4). And we need to remember this when all is dark and we seem to be doing little more than dodging the arrows of the wicked (v. 2).

So what is Psalm 11 saying to us? It is saying that faith needs discernment to filter out counsels of despair and fear; faith needs vision to see the just and reigning God; and faith needs hope that anticipates awaking and gazing on his face. All this should prove of real help—when everything falls apart.

PSALM 12

For the music leader. Upon the sheminith. A psalm of David.

1 Save, Yahweh, for covenant man is no more,
   for faithful ones have vanished from the sons of men.
2 Empty talk is what they speak, each one, with his neighbor;
   with smooth talk, with a double heart they speak.
3 May Yahweh cut off all smooth talkers,
   the tongue making boastful claims,
4 ones who say, 'With our tongue we will dominate;
   our lips are with us; who is master over us?'

5 'Because of the violence done to the afflicted,
   because of the groaning that comes from the needy,
   now I will rise up,' says Yahweh,
   'I will place him in the safety for which he longs.'
6 The words of Yahweh are pure words,
   silver refined in a furnace on earth,
   purified seven times.

7 You, Yahweh, will keep them,
   you will preserve him from this generation forever.
8 Wicked folks strut around all over the place
   when vileness is exalted among the sons of men.

SPIN DOCTORS

12

Paul Johnson says that at the age of 89 Frank Lloyd Wright testified in the witness-box that he was 'the greatest architect in the world.' His wife informed him that modesty would have been more effective, but Wright retorted, 'You forget that I was under oath.' Most folks are not that scrupulous for the truth, I suppose! Indeed, David laments (and we don't know the exact setting in which he did so) a society wholly taken over by the lie, where he met deception, flattery, arrogance, and falsehood at every turn. One could easily imagine David thinking this way during all the hooks and crooks of Absalom's rebellion in 2 Samuel 15–18—but we simply can't be sure. But the pattern in the psalm is easy to trace: where we are (vv 1–4); what we hear (vv 5–6); and, how we get on (vv 7–8). Psalm 12 poses the question: What can God's people do when the spin doctors win? And we must begin by trying to discern how far the lie has gone...

A lying society

First, David places before us a lying society (vv. 1–4). And we need to pick apart the text to get a grip on what he depicts for us. He first points us to a peculiar *absence* (v. 1)—'covenant man is no more,' 'faithful ones have vanished.' 'Covenant man' is my paraphrase of the adjective *hasid*, referring to those who have received Yahweh's *hesed*, his faithful love, and who respond to him in faithful love. Yahweh's faithful people are not around. David does not say why or how they have vanished—simply that they have. We may not think too much about this, but *a la* Matthew 5:13, when the 'salt' is gone (not so much the agent that preserves but one that retards spoilage) there is nothing to prevent or 'put the brakes on' decay and rottenness.

If verse 1 tells us what, or who, isn't there, verse 2 tells us what is there—he describes the social *trend*. And it all centers on speech, speech that is nothing but emptiness ('empty talk,' i.e., no substance to it, no foundation in fact), flattery ('smooth talk'), and deception ('double heart'). This problem is not occasional but pervasive, since 'each one' talks this way with his neighbor. All this erupts in an urgent *prayer* (v. 3) that Yahweh would 'cut off' such deceivers, who are driven by their arrogant *philosophy* (v. 4) that they can 'take all' simply by their clever word-smithing. Welcome to the lying society, where speech is empty, flattering, deceptive, and arrogant.

And today—have we a lying society? One hardly needs to ask. We run into lying advertising. Of course we expect this; we know we're being conned. We've put up with it for so long that we expect nothing different. It even involves our hamburgers. Eric Clark tells of Burger King once running an ad in which a girl complains that McDonald's burgers were 20% smaller than Burger King's. Of course, she neglected to say that BK's cost 20% more. Sometimes the deception rests in what is not said.

We likewise expect to face lying politics. All the way from small sound bites to general 'image.' On his last trip to France, Richard Nixon told a crowd at the airport that forty years before he had 'majored in French,' took four years of it, could then speak it, write it, but now—years later—he could understand only a little. Actually he had majored in history—but he had wanted to massage the French. Seymour Hersh reminds Americans of the image cut by John Kennedy as the attentive husband and family man, the hard-working chief executive, spending night hours poring over government reports. But his Secret Service agents knew what he often did at night or other times—when they would have to watch a door because a sex-obsessed president was behind it with two hookers. He was a 'devoted' family man who took his VD to the grave with him.

And once we may have expected a higher standard with the media than with advertising and politics. But not now. Over twenty years ago (in *Prodigal Press*) Marvin Olasky told of a *New York Daily News* reporter who admitted that he had made up 'facts' when reporting on violence in Northern Ireland; that reporter defended himself by saying he had done the same thing three hundred times before. And the *New York Times* had to acknowledge that it had published an article about a trip inside Cambodia by a writer who had not gone to Cambodia. 'Empty talk..., each one, with his neighbor.'

We might suppose that in our judicial systems we could surely expect to find truth. But there we run into legal lying. A stint spent in jury duty can give one a fresh sense of realism. Robert Caro tells of the 1948 Senate election in the state of Texas. Lyndon Johnson 'won' the election by eighty-seven votes out of about a million cast. The election was stolen. There were hearings, a thousand pages of court transcripts. The election judge in the crucial precinct in Jim Wells County testified the opposite of all the other people. His name was Luis Salas. Caro interviewed him in 1986 and asked him about his contrary testimony. His response was: 'Well that's simple, Robert. I lied under oath.'

Nor does the setting have to be secular—we are becoming quite used to religious lying. One doesn't have to turn on religious television programming to find it. Sometimes it's closer to home. Kent Hughes tells of a friend of his who was pastor of a small church. He confided to Hughes that his slim salary was inadequate and that he could not continue in ministry unless he received help. Kent Hughes wrote him a $2,000 check from his personal account. He found out later that this 'friend' had scammed at least $50,000 from others with the same 'song and dance.'

Government lying, of course, has long been a thriving trade. You may begin to think that you will get closer to the truth from those people news reports mention in that delightful turn of phrase—'speaking on condition of anonymity because not authorized to discuss officially.' When the Bolsheviks seized power in what would become the Soviet Union, evangelical believers could not see where communism was going to lead. They knew their country lay under economic woe and government corruption and they were somewhat heartened by a statement quoted from

Lenin that 'each person must have complete freedom not only to observe any faith but also to propagate any faith' and that 'none of the officials should even have a right to ask anyone of his faith...nobody should dare to interfere in this field' (cited in James and Marti Hefley's *By Their Blood*). And then thousands upon thousands of believers are flushed into the great Soviet sewage system. But it makes little difference if regimes are totalitarian or democratic—the lie is their *technique du jour*. We are used to it; it doesn't surprise us. Indeed, Carl Jung once said, 'No nation keeps its word'—no need to retract that anytime soon. The spin doctors are always at work.

> Save, Yahweh, for covenant man is no more,
> for faithful ones have vanished from the sons of men.
> Empty talk is what they speak, each one, with his neighbor;
> with smooth talk, with a double heart they speak.

A pure word

But, secondly, we meet other words in this psalm, indeed, a pure word (vv. 5-6). Here is a word from Yahweh himself! Some think the words of verse 5 may have come to David through a prophet serving at the sanctuary, but we simply don't know. They may have been an assurance given directly to David as the prophet-psalmist.

Note that verse 5 consists of Yahweh's assurance to his desperate people and is given in the first person ('...now I will rise up...I will place him in the safety for which he longs'), while verse 6 is an assurance about that assurance, that is, it underscores the character of Yahweh's word, that there is no dross, impurity, or deception in it (in complete contrast to the verbiage thrown around in verses 1–4). So verse 6 simply says that you can totally, utterly, absolutely rely on Yahweh's words in verse 5. You have come, as it were, from a truth-twisting society in verses 1–4 to stand before a truth-speaking God in verse 5.

We need to understand Yahweh's assurance in verse 5: 'Because of the violence done to the afflicted, because of the groaning that comes from the needy, now I will rise up.' Yahweh is saying he is responding to the sufferings of his people (the 'afflicted' and 'needy') and that he is going to relieve them. But now, what do we make of this 'now'? 'Now I will rise up.' This 'now' may not be immediate, as verses 7–8 seem to show. In those next verses Yahweh preserves his people in the meantime but it looks like the wicked are still 'strutting their stuff,' as we say (v. 8). In fact, the verb in verse 5 that I have translated as a present, 'says,' might more strictly be translated as an English future, 'will say.' So verse 5 may well be relating what Yahweh 'will say' at that time when he is ready to bring final, decisive deliverance to his people. The stress is not on the immediacy of the relief but on the certainty of the word.

The contrast should grab us: after wading through the slick double-speak and deliberate deception of a lie-infatuated world (vv. 1–4) we come to a seeing and hearing (see 5a) and truth-speaking God (5b–6). What an immense relief to have a steadfast God in the midst of all the falsehoods and infidelities of life as we know it. I like the story Donald Grey Barnhouse told of the famed Spanish Escorial outside Madrid. It includes an Augustinian monastery and a magnificent church. The architect who designed the building made an arch so flat that it frightened the king. So the king ordered the architect to add a column which would support the middle of the arch. The architect argued that it was not necessary, but the king insisted, as kings tend to do. The column was built. Years later the king died, as kings also tend to do, and the architect revealed that the column was a quarter of an inch shy of the arch, and that the arch had never sagged in the slightest. Barnhouse said that guides would pass a lath between the arch and the column as silent proof of the architect's word.

Hence Yahweh's servants lean hard upon his promises. If they wonder how they will fare at the last, they rest on the assurance that 'Yahweh redeems the life of his servants; none of those who take refuge in him will be condemned' (Ps. 34:22). If they are longing for the full coming of the kingdom the dogmatism of Psalm 46:10 settles them: 'I will be exalted among the nations; I will be exalted in the earth.' If they fear they may be cast aside, they take fresh heart when they hear 'Yahweh will not forsake his people; he will not abandon his heritage' (Ps. 94:14).

A present paradox

Finally, we meet a present paradox at the close of the psalm (vv. 7–8). Note what you find here. You have a *clear confidence* in verse 7 ('You, Yahweh, will keep them, you will preserve him from this generation forever'). The idea seems to be that Yahweh will guard and preserve his people from the lying generation even before the decisive 'now' of verse 5 arrives. Verse 7 is really a response of faith to the content of verses 5–6. And yet you also meet a *present reality* in verse 8 ('Wicked folks strut around all over the place...'). Verse 8 seems to depict the situation of verses 1–4 and suggests that it still continues. The world view of the wicked still seems to carry the day. So, do you sense the tension and paradox side-by-side? Yahweh preserves us (7) and yet crud rules the day (8).

We don't particularly like paradoxes, though the Christian life is full of them. William Guthrie (d. 1665) left us with a frightening one on his death-bed. Faith Cook writes about him; he was only forty-five, but his health broke, and his end was very hard. He suffered such violent pains that his friends were forced to hold him down. Between the attacks of pain he summoned the strength to say, 'Though I should die mad, yet I know I shall die in the Lord.' That is a bit hard to hold together. As if to say: 'My pain may drive me out of my mind, but it cannot drive me out of Christ.'

And we are left with a tension and a paradox at the close of this psalm. We do not know how severe our troubles may be if the wicked still have tenure to swagger and strut (v. 8); we only know that in and in spite of that Yahweh will keep and preserve his people (v. 7). And with that assurance we can press on until the time of Yahweh's 'now' arrives.